C.-F. Ramuz

WHAT IS MAN

Translation by Gouverneur Paulding
Introduction by Albert Béguin

Pantheon Books

BY THE SAME AUTHOR

THE END OF ALL MEN
WHEN THE MOUNTAIN FELL

Printed in the U. S. A.
by Belgrave Press, New York, N. Y.

EDITOR'S NOTE

This book combines extracts from three titles:
Besoin de Grandeur, Taille de l'Homme, Questions.

Permission to present these three volumes in selections was given by C.-F. Ramuz shortly before his death.

SOURCES

INTRODUCTION

Charles-Ferdinand Ramuz was one of the best novelists and also one of the most lucid commentators on the crisis of our times. Yet nothing could have been less eventful than his private life. He was born in Switzerland on September 24, 1878. His parents, of peasant origin, kept a little shop in Lausanne. He had a city childhood and only went to the country for holidays. In school he kept aloof from companions and, although he excelled at literature, instinctively rebelled against the theoretical side of his education. He was already in search of a more direct contact with the concrete, with life itself. Nor did he ever, even as a grown man, enjoy argument for its own sake, on an abstract plane. Yet he was inherently religious and troubled, from youth on, by metaphysical questions.

Entering the university at eighteen, he quietly set to work, without real enthusiasm, for his degree of Licencié ès Lettres. Normally, this would have led straight into teaching, but to teach meant to become an employee of the State and Ramuz had no wish to be a bureaucrat. His nature demanded so complete an independence that at times it was close to anarchical. He dreaded fixed habits and routine. At first he wanted to paint, but it was not long before he began to write and soon he felt that this was his true vocation.

Like all authors in those days, he started with tragedies in classic verse, but of these none have survived. He was twenty-five when his first collection of poems was published at his own expense. Needing money, he felt obliged to take a position as tutor. He went to Weimar, where he was profoundly bored, and a few months of teaching in his own country bored him still more. Determined, thereafter, to devote himself entirely to writing, in 1902 he set forth, with a small subsidy from his father, for Paris.

Ramuz, who traveled little, never loved but two settings: his small Swiss province on the shores of Lake Léman, and Paris. It seemed to Ramuz that the same kind of grandeur could be found in both mountains and metropolis—the same grandeur and, too, the same sense of solitude, to which he was drawn by instinct, by timidity and pride. He spent some twelve years in

Paris, only returning to Switzerland for the summer vacations—to lose himself in some remote village. Throughout these twelve years he knew practically no other writers and never frequented literary circles. For months at a time he spoke to no one except his concierge or his grocer in Montparnasse, and only became sociable when he chanced upon childhood friends from his own land. It was during this period that he published his early novels. "Aline," the first, was a masterpiece, but, for some time, only a few writers took notice of this talent in the making.

It was not disappointed ambition, however, that decided Ramuz to return home a few months before the war of 1914. More and more deeply, as he continued to write about the life of the Swiss peasant, he had become aware of his roots and of his inability to transplant them to the French capital. This feeling was wholly logical. Both his Protestant training, in which the Bible took the place held in France by the classic authors, and his provincial inarticulacy in the face of the Parisian fluency of speech, accentuated his feeling of exile. But, above all, the combination of his peasant ancestry and his own nature had given Ramuz an inherent love of the concrete, and a need to search for fundamentals which kept him from adapting himself to the kind of intellectualism and the modern tempo characteristic of a great city.

From 1914 until his death in 1947, Ramuz lived on his own plot of ground, leaving it only for the briefest excursions to Paris at his editor's request. He married, he had a daughter, he worked. For a long time he lived in great poverty, accepting it as the price of a writer's independence. Each year he published another book. During the war of 1914 he gathered round him a few young writers and some painters who seemed quite revolutionary in this very conservative country. His most productive friendship was with Igor Stravinsky. Through his long collaboration with Stravinsky, during which he wrote the text for both "Noces" and "L'Histoire du Soldat," Ramuz was introduced to modern esthetics and a broader knowledge of the world. He read the Russian novelists; he followed closely the events of 1917; he found out that in learning to understand the nature of man in his own country, he could discover the nature of all mankind.

It was in this period that one of the guiding principles of Ramuz took shape: the belief that there is a changeless element in man, antedating his civilization, based on his intrinsic freedom, his sense of worship, and his participation in the life of nature. He came to believe that man's increasing ability to acquire knowledge by reason estranges him and cuts him off from his most basic self. He therefore concluded that the only salvation lay in the abandonment of intellectualism. Rather than admitting, with the rationalists, that what unites men is the general, he believed that the only living truth is the particular. This was to be the dominating theme of his art, and also of his humanism. His entire work as novelist and essayist is an attempt to prove that the man most deeply rooted in a particular soil, most faithful to his particular origin, will be able to reach the closest understanding with men of different origin. For it is the elementary in man that is common to all. These views have nothing to do with a philosophy or a doctrine; they are the views of an artist; they are one man's experience. Ramuz held to them more and more firmly as his life went on.

This does not mean that the stay-at-home Ramuz was shut off from the outside world. He was far more alive to the world than many a cosmopolitan traveler. The decision to ignore a certain kind of culture did not mean that he took refuge in ignorance. And although he made it a point of pride to pretend that he knew nothing, Ramuz kept abreast of every development. He read a great deal in many fields, following with as much interest the progress of science as of literature; for example, his novels were among the earliest to show the influence of motion-picture techniques, for he understood the positive value of such discoveries. And although, in his youth, he seemed to have been absorbed by his personal concerns, the war of 1914 aroused his interest in political and social problems. Enlarging the scope of his novels, he began to give a broader picture of groups and whole communities of men. At the same time he wrote articles for the Swiss newspapers, in which he was able to express his reflections on the war, the peace, the changes in society, and the opportunity to establish justice and freedom. In 1917, he enthusiastically greeted the first Russian Revolution (the Republican Revolution in May) in a short book entitled "The Great Spring" (Le Grand Printemps). But in the following years his novels had a certain apocalyptic tone revealing profound distress. A phase of somber mysticism marked his thinking at that time and he would return repeatedly to the same subject: catastrophe and the end of the world.

Meanwhile his reputation had spread. First recognized by the greatest writers of his time, by Claudel, Gide and Valéry, the Swiss novelist began at last to see his books reach the general public, and at the threshold of fifty, having written some twenty important books, he could be reasonably sure for the first time of material security for himself and his family.

In the great political crisis of the 1930's, many of the younger generation turned to him for spiritual guidance. It was during this period that, without giving up his novel-writing, he produced the important studies, selections from which compose this book: "Taille de l'Homme" (Man's Stature) in 1933, "Questions" in 1935, "Besoin de Grandeur" (Need of Grandeur) in 1937. These books have not aged, for they are still readable today, after all the destruction of our world. They are still entirely valid for, strictly speaking, they are not political books which would have been outdated by events. In these studies Ramuz always speaks as a poet, a mind that can see beyond appearances to the enduring human values and distinguish the permanent from the ephemeral. But he is not an aristocratic poet of the intellect; he has no wish to bring to the fundamental problems of life the subtleties of intellect or culture. On the contrary, with no compromise whatever nor any desire to popularize his ideas, but simply because it is natural to him, Ramuz obstinately confines himself to asking the questions that all men ask themselves. Where others turn to scientific analysis and the hypotheses of philosophical systems, Ramuz deliberately ignores this acquired knowledge and returns to elementals. He is quite as well able as anyone else to discuss economics with economists, theories with theoreticians, ideologies with ideologists; but such matters belong to another plane, a plane that is not his. His is the realm of simplicity.

What preoccupies Ramuz is the disquiet, conscious or unconscious, of the man in the street. The questions he asks center round the great commonplaces: What is man? What are his needs? How can he be saved from his solitude? How can he create a society which will not be inimical to him, which will not destroy what is most valuable in him? How can he reconcile the demands of freedom with those of law and order? Is there such a thing as equality? And where is there room for love in the world of today, for the sacred, for God Himself? If there is no room left for love, for the sacred, for God, can man

14

alone have any hope of creating peace and happiness, a paradise on earth?

These are almost childlike questions, yet they are fundamental. Ramuz faces the modern world not as a reactionary who denies the changing times through inertia, but simply as a man who is asking himself "What does it all mean?" In no sense a doctrinaire, he merely asks questions; he asks them to trouble and rouse man's sleeping anxiety, to remind man of the need for vigilance. For us of the twentieth century, the optimism of the past hundred years is no longer permissible; the events of our time, the wars, revolutions and tyrannies, the political, economic and social crises, have shaken all established values. This total upheaval challenges not only the values of yesterday and the hopes of our fathers, but the values commonly accepted in all the civilizations that have ever existed—in ancient times as well as in the era of Christianity and liberalism. Is this the end of a world, the end of the world? Is it the dawn of a new humanity? Is there to be a better or a worse humanity?

The Ramuz who is anguished and invites us to share his anguish is a man with a long tradition behind him. He has remained a peasant in spite of his anarchy as an artist, and centuries of in-

15

herited experience have taught him the advantages of peasant life. Pagan or Christian, Chinese, Russian or Swiss, the peasant has always kept a sense of balance, a special kind of freedom, a harmonious relationship with nature, and when he has had to face dangers, these dangers were tempered to fit him. For a long time man's conception of the universe bore some relation to himself; there was no disproportion between creature and creation; God alone was infinite, but He gave the promise of harmony between man and the world about him. But the evolution of reason has changed this relationship and, in recent times, the cry uttered by Pascal upon discovering the infinite universe of modern science has been repeated from generation to generation. Ramuz, in turn, has given tongue to his anxiety that man should no longer have a "stature" of his own in the boundless immensity of the universe. But this anguish, which is metaphysical, is related to the evolution of human society. For in this, too, the small community which fitted each individual into a world made to his measure has given way to the vast organism of the modern state. What can become of man now caught in these mechanical states, and unable to see them as a whole? Moreover, just as the political structure of society is undergoing a transformation, so, too, the inventions of the scientist and the engineer are completely changing the relationship between man and matter, between man and man. Not only are the conditions of labor different, but even the meaning of work itself has altered, for it is less and less satisfying to the individual, less and less a happy creation of one man alone. The pattern of change is uniform and once again the question must be asked: in this new scheme of life, can man still be himself?

For anyone who cares to ask, contemporary history provides its own contradictory answers and its spectacle of catastrophe. But at the time Ramuz began to touch upon these inevitable problems, he saw three struggles toward a solution undertaken: first, Russian communism, which for fifteen years had been attempting to master technology and to base society on a new notion of justice and the community. Second, throughout the West and in America, liberal capitalism, moving steadily toward state centralization and planned economy. And a third experiment, launched by Hitler and Mussolini, whose brave new world had not yet revealed all its criminal instincts, but already denied both justice and freedom. Some saw in fascism a logical and inevi-

table decadence of bourgeois democracy, others viewed it as a variant of communism.

What would be the position of Ramuz? With no sympathy for any of them, he yet refused to make a sweeping condemnation of them all. In communism he recognized the search for justice and the roused instinct for revolutionary progress that could restore men's hopes; but he also saw that communism completely abolished all known manifestations of the sacred. He had nothing but horror for fascist solutions, having seen their scandalous results, but even in fascism he believed that he could detect a certain fundamental need, however terribly distorted, for grandeur. As for Western capitalism, this system, too, seemed to him to wound man's religious sense and to cripple his real freedom, though it made room for a relative freedom non-existent in the other regimes.

The reader must not expect to find in Ramuz either new solutions or any form of political allegiance. This was not his mission. And for that matter who is there today who could offer answers to the real questions, even presupposing the courage to raise them at all? Ramuz knew that his role was to be the poet in our world. He had no idea of replacing the politician or the econ-

*omist; he wanted to speak to the depths of our
individual souls and to remind us of those eternal
desires or rights which were being stifled. It was
not a question for Ramuz of turning back, of
denying material progress; he had no nostalgia
for the old, bygone order of things. In judging,
he bore in mind a humanity not of yesterday, nor
of today, nor even of tomorrow, but an eternal
humanity—man, as he is and always will be, inspired or downcast, in light or in shadow, in hope
or in defeat. Misery and grandeur, solitude and
unity, enslavement to the soil and a freedom that
is almost anarchy, conservatism and revolution:
these paradoxes, these contradictory elements,
according to Ramuz, are the eternal constituents
of human life. The poet discovers man's nature
through a long process of questioning. But in the
background are always the final, the all-important questions to which the poet Ramuz returned
throughout his reflective writing for, though he
confessed no formal faith, Ramuz was essentially
religious. Will modern man deny God and succeed in living without Him? Will he succeed in
severing himself from his entire spiritual heri-
tage? Would such a breaking off be possible?
Might it not even prove fatal, might it not doom
the world to death? Possibly man can only keep*

a "stature," a place in the world, by not dismissing God and thus a whole part of himself.

In all humility Ramuz left it to the future to answer this question. He did not feel more than the right to ask it: to keep alive the saving grace of anxiety in man.

Albert Béguin

WHAT IS MAN

IT HAS BEEN my lot, alas, to write books, but writing is not my trade. I started out with painting. By this I mean that from youth what I wanted to do, strangely enough, was to try to reproduce not ideas but objects, and I wanted to endow the images I made of these objects with a certain likeness to the objects, of course, but also to myself. A flower, a mountain, a face, a table, just as the painter sees them—only the painter uses color.

The painter is lucky enough to have a technique all his own. To express himself he uses colored pastes or liquids which he sets side by side, or one on top of the other, spreading them with a brush on canvas or paper. You do not paint spontaneously the way you speak; you are obliged to learn (or someone has to teach you) how to use this special language. My misfortune has been to use a language that is available to everybody.

23

For it happens that words are everybody's property; words, and also the way to use them, that is to say the way you bring them together, combine them, subordinate one to another, and thus form a phrase; you group together things that are alive and separate, and then the group lives also. Everyone is capable of making phrases (good or bad ones) but relatively few people can paint a picture.

My mistake (if I may speak about myself, yet I am compelled to do so) was to choose a means of expression perhaps unsuited to me and furthermore a means used by everyone. Attempting to paint, I talk; in talking, I try to paint. But everyone talks (in this case it is of little importance whether we are discussing the written or the spoken language, for today everybody writes and everybody has learned how to write). A painter commits himself infinitely less when he paints than a writer when he writes, and this is precisely because everybody writes and very few people paint. The painter, just because he has this special means of expressing himself, lives in a privileged and restricted world; the writer lives in everybody's world, in a world where everybody —including the writer—has equal privileges and competency.

24

It may happen occasionally that a painter and a writer, each in his own technique, each expressing his own individual nature, nonetheless show that they both belong to exactly the same psychological type. The public does not care whether they do or not; the public is not concerned with psychological types; the public does not see beyond the difference in techniques; it sees, therefore, a far greater likeness between Giotto and Rembrandt (since both of them paint) than between Racine and Poussin (because one is a writer, the other a painter).

Hence the public's peculiar treatment of the writer: demanding an accounting from the writer, but from the painter none at all.

It is not in half-measures that the writer commits himself. The degree of self-revelation is not something that the writer can decide and limit. The painter reveals what he wants to reveal, and the public, because the painter paints pictures, does not insist on more; whereas because the writer's tools are everybody's tools, he is forced to a complete self-revelation—otherwise he soon ceases to be a writer; he becomes a "problem," that is, a kind of enigma which at first arouses curiosity, attracts the curious, but then discourages and irritates them. The writer who seems obscure to his public—for one reason or another, and it is not always his fault—soon finds himself called upon to explain what he is after, or be completely abandoned by his readers. "We do not understand," the public says—and gives up. The writer may surprise, or shock, or be difficult, but only provided his public is rewarded in the end for the trouble to which he has put it; that is to say, provided the writer manages ultimately to convince or persuade. At the very least the writer must show where he stands in relation to the positions taken by the groups of opinion —of every kind of opinion—which surround him; particularly, nowadays, the position taken by political groups. For in our times men are concerned primarily with politics, for obvious reasons. This concern with politics is aggravated by a curious phenomenon of polarization: in politics only the poles are active. You have to belong to the "Left" or to the "Right." A man's talents, or gifts, which alone should count, soon will no longer matter at all: in other words, the "Right" backs its own men and the "Left" does the same, whether or not they are talented or gifted. And if the time has not yet come when the first and only question put to a painter is whether he is Left or Right, that is now the first and only question

asked of the writer. The writer's mistake is that
he uses words, not colors. "Words belong to me
as much as they do to him," says the reader, "he
puts words in front of me and it is to me that he
is speaking. What is he trying to say? Is he for
or against me?"

I am a painter, but I write; that is my mistake.
I want to be considered a painter and I have no
right to ask people to think of me as a painter,
because I have no palette. The distinction is clear
in Pascal's phrase: "They seek to stir, not to
teach." I want to stir, and nothing else, but it is
only the painters who have the right to stir and
nothing else. It is in vain that the writer makes
no claim to teach; people still persist in looking
for the lesson in what he writes. That is because
the writer uses words. Whether he wants to be or
not, the writer nowadays is immediately classified; by the critics, by the reader, and even by
those who have not read him—classified according to the "message" that people find, or think
they find, in his work. He is even classified simultaneously in all sorts of contradictory categories
—a fact which he may find personally reassuring
but which tends to add to the confusion. A writer
may be known, at one and the same time, as both
a communist and a Catholic. He takes his charac-

ters from the "people"—a word, for instance, which he detests—and that is enough to make him a communist. His style is considered "revolutionary": the next step is quickly taken and he himself is called revolutionary. But at the same time his work shows "humble objectivity" (in the jargon) or again there is "a sense of mystery," a certain need for the absolute and the universal, which is also in his work, and for this he will be adopted by certain Catholics—to his extreme astonishment.

It has taken me a long while to find out that to be alone is a great luxury, a luxury that must be paid for dearly, that has always cost a great deal, but that is going to cost more and more; a luxury all the more expensive in that the writer does not choose it: it is forced upon him. For if he does not rally to a group, it is not in the least through ill-will on his part as people often think; it is because he is surrounded by people who know, whereas he knows that he knows nothing. He is placed among people who affirm, whereas he interrogates; and those who affirm are followers of Someone with a capital S or just someone, while the writer's interrogations are prompted by no one, for when you ask questions you only ask your own questions. He is not in the least what you call a "sceptic"; he hopes he will end by knowing; he only realizes that for the moment he does not know. But at the same time he is well aware that questions interest no one; that answers are what are avidly desired by everyone today, answers and not questions; and that when one has no answers to give one had better be silent.

He sees also that words carry positive, unexpected implications even when all he intended to do was to make them ask questions. He sees that by asking questions he could not avoid presenting objects and beings, causing them to affect each other in a certain way determined by himself, creating certain relationships between them, a self-revealing relationship chosen by himself; and he finds that here already is a positive viewpoint for which he is responsible. He sees that unwittingly he has taken one direction rather than another, and that it is no longer in his power to prevent the reader from following him. He perceives, finally (and this is a graver matter as he looks back in severe self-examination), that he has often left the world of concrete objects in order to visit—he, too, against his will—the world of ideas; with the result that the public is not alone responsible for the misunderstanding.

And now young Protestants come to him and say: "You are a Protestant?"

He says: "No."

"But you were born a Protestant?"

He says: "Yes."

"Then you cannot get away from your education. You are one of us."

Thus he ends by seeing that he is Catholic, that he is communist, that he is Protestant (to his great astonishment), but his astonishment is still greater when he discovers, upon reflection, that possibly he is all three at once.

Or at least he sees that these various systems presuppose solutions which, one after another, or all together, have seriously attracted him, and therefore the first thing to find out is whether they are contradictory or whether, viewed at a certain angle, they may not be able to work together, each bringing its own share, to form a general solution.

First of all you have to realize this: the writer, the imaginative writer, the poet, is a man without personal existence—precisely because of his imagination. He constantly goes out of himself, loses himself, to enter completely the image with

which he is then occupied: that of a character,
for instance, with whom he wholly identifies himself, since he puts his own life into the character's life—the only way to make a character live
—or that of an object which begins to have real
existence within the writer only after it has
caused him to lose all sense of his own existence.

The attitude of the poet to an idea is quite different from that of the logician. The logician pro-
gresses step by step; he decides that an idea is
true, he takes possession of one idea, then of another, and associates the two, proceeding from
cause to cause or from result to result. The logician is never inactive, the logician acts. But the
poet is passive; lovingly he contemplates whole
clusters of ideas which he sees in patterns, and is
drawn to them because they are patterns. The
poet fastens himself to them and then draws
apart; he does not take a stand; he can love opposites; he lets himself be acted upon.

The poet's responsibility should therefore be
of another order than that of the logician: and
this certainly is a point on which everyone agrees
or, at least, used to agree, in reasonable times. But
today times no longer are reasonable. The mind,
the heart, and all our needs together, search in
confusion for the truth. The need to eat, the need

for shelter, the need for warmth (literal and figurative), the need for security—and not for the body alone, since there is no longer any distinction between the needs of body, heart, or mind—the need to believe, and at the same time to know and to understand—for no one wants to see, or gives himself the time to see, that the need to believe is not the same as the need to understand—all these diverse activities, of wisdom, science, poetry and also religion, hasten along their different paths, all at the same time, toward the same goal, which is the common goal of knowledge.

That is why the poet is compromised, for poetry is also an activity, and people put questions to the poet who himself is putting questions, and they expect the poet to furnish answers, whereas he wants only to ask questions.

This process of interrogation stirs men, but in the kind of world we live in you do not stir men's emotions without also arousing their thirst for knowledge; for it is from knowledge that everyone nowadays awaits the bettering of his lot. As a result the poet is condemned to silence or else he, too, is condemned to become a doctor—though he is himself so ill. Yet a man is a poet only because he is so ill, for there is no poetry when everything is going well. Swathed in bandages, lame, hobbling on crutches though he is, he is still surrounded by beggars, other beggars, lamer than he, hobbling with greater difficulty on their crutches, more pitifully disfigured, in greater distress—and who have already tried so many remedies.

The real doctor is powerless; he can bind wounds, yet he cannot cure. But everyone awaits a miracle: an instantaneous and general recovery, a universal cure for disease, a collective resurrection.

Nevertheless, people will finally have to realize that, more often than not, there is no connection between what a man is and what he thinks, or supposes he thinks. There can be, for instance, far greater and far more real kinship between a divine-right Monarchist and a militant Communist (to remain in the realm of political opinion) than between two French Radical-Socialists of the same hue.

A man generally finds his ideas ready-made; he owes them to circumstance, not to himself. He changes his ideas without changing himself. And through ideas he expresses his passions, his needs, his hatreds, his fears, his interests, but not himself. Consider the fact that Germany, all Germany, turned Socialist in the course of a few autumn days in 1918, and that this same Germany is at present ninety percent Nazi. This case, it will be said, is extreme; it is only extremely obvious. Anyone attempting to think directly, with an entirely personal purity, first of all must "be"; but the fact is that few men have true "being." Most men exist socially, not personally; their ideas are derivative and not their own. Man defends himself; his "ideas" serve primarily to defend him. Class defends itself against class, party against party. Doctrinal unity masks an extreme physiological diversity. People rarely think in any other way than socially; in other words, they do not think at all. In order to think fully a man must first make a clean sweep of all preconceived ideas, accepting ideas only after carefully checking them one by one and testing them for their authentic relationship to his own being. After all, that is what Descartes had done when he said: "I think, hence I am." You cannot do your thinking second-hand.

But, alas, how can we look into our consciousness and separate the inherent from the accidental; what we have made ourselves from what has been handed down to us ready-made; what expresses our true being from what expresses only our social being. Ready-made ideas lie about in newspapers, in books, in conversations; men pick them up to suit their immediate interests, which may not be those of tomorrow, and their needs of today, which will change just as rapidly. When their needs change, men change their ideas, naively and with a total lack of embarrassment.

Ideas do not express man; if they did, you would recognize the atheist in the street, and also the man with a faith. Generally, the religious man is religious only because his family is religious; generally, the atheist is an atheist only because his friends are atheists. Ideas are a ready-made suit which man puts on to cover his nakedness, a suit which he does not even buy and wear out, but which he simply rents. You see him dressed by turns in red, in khaki, in brown. Man, nowadays, is nothing but a shirt. Who cares any more about the human being, about what forms real human substance as you sometimes find it expressed in a book, not through ideas alone, but in the living tissue of the words, the juxtaposition of phrases, their emotional armature? Yet this is how direct contact is made with a certain reality, with stars, plants, animals, water, the earth, the skies.

Ideas are the occupational disease of the great cities which an over-civilization has set apart from the wholeness of life, creating an intense but one-sided life within the cities, in which nothing exists outside social consciousness—these cities in which man acts as master of all things and of himself—until some great cataclysm comes to shock him out of his blindness.

Yet there have been periods in which a certain conception of the world was completely accepted, so universally that no one, at least openly, thought of questioning it. It was a conception based on authority; it proceeded from certain accepted dogmas. Within this frame of reference man, metaphysically, was something definite, from which to deduce certain sociological, political or physiological consequences. Those were deductive periods, periods in which everything started from above. You could call them "periodic," for their metaphysics had a repercussion even on the language: periods when men expressed themselves in periodic sentences, and not in books alone, but also in all public or private documents and even personal letters. Everything was written in the same style, a style based on a main clause round which a great number of subordinate clauses took up their ordered positions, in varied but always strictly preordained relationship. The hierarchy of principles was immutable. The principal, the dominant, was in its place. Today it is exactly the opposite. The design was preestablished; there was an abstract conception of the objects to be arranged, and of their positions; but today that conception is lacking. We are completely impressionist in everything. We meekly yield to successive and contradictory impressions and our only hope is that the sum total will somehow reconstitute the image of reality. It is difficult to see which of these impressions is essential; you cannot see the dominant, for all are on the same plane, and it is therefore possible to select any one of them as a foundation—which is obviously what everyone is now doing.

The sociologist builds on sociology, the political thinker on politics, the scientist on his science; but the theologian, who could say we build on God, is silent. For no one builds on God (Who was the principal element in the periodic system because He was the Principle), yet everyone ends by reaching God, or by attempting to reach God.

37

In other words, we reason from the particular to the general, starting out from wherever our profession, our social position or our occupation has placed us. The system is completely inductive and totally anarchical. Fortunately for law and order, however, political parties, ideologies, and also the willingness of most men to accept a slogan, have so far held in check the elements of incoherence and violence this system contains.

Once the writer has revealed himself, however little, he is trapped; either he must stop writing altogether, or continue to surrender more and more of his privacy. He is called upon for explanations and he is quite aware that this questioning is not unjustifiable, for he sees clearly that he may not have sufficiently explained himself to himself.

"Well then, who are you?" he asks himself. "Are you a coherent person or an incoherent person? You live, or at any rate you claim to be alive, since you express yourself. What is the center of your existence? Has that center always been the same, or has it changed? If it has changed, then have you changed too? But what made you change? Did the change come suddenly, or little by little?"

Writer, know thyself.

Could it be that man is no more than a body—with an identity card? But an identity card is only a name, a date of birth, a place of birth, with the parents' names, a father, a mother; it records only causes and their result: a man. It is a point of departure facing a blank space (do not write here) on which the point of arrival has still to be written, and you may be sure that this blank space will some day be filled. (This is the one thing of which you may be certain.)

But there is something between the points of departure and arrival: man himself. What does the identity card tell about him?

For a long time, while I was still a little boy, I thought I should never die. It was plain that people round me died, but that did not alter my conviction: I myself was not made to die. I must have been seven or eight. At that age children often engage in protracted metaphysical meditations of which their parents are usually entirely unaware and at which, if they happened to perceive them, they would doubtless only laugh. The child is still essentially undisciplined (inwardly); he is still shapeless, he is trying to find a shape. There is, of course, the shape people propose to give him, or impose upon him, and this is almost always the shape he finally acquires. But the child, at least in the beginning, only appears to accept it, while actually stealing away, escaping time after time into his private meditations. He is still aware that he has a personal existence, an idea which school, parents and society will take it upon themselves to disprove. The child is still infinitely naive (in the literal sense) and there are many things which, though later he would not admit them even to himself, he now contemplates with candid cynicism. He is not yet, as they say, "inhibited"; he has not yet given in to the world's cowardice. He is seven or eight, and he tells himself that for sure he will not die; that even if everyone has to die, he will not die.

I remember very well how I used to shut myself up in the barn where my father kept his wine casks. The barn stood at the edge of the garden so that when I entered it I had the garden behind me, with a fountain, a chestnut tree, flowers, and beyond, in the neighbors' gardens that you could see spread out one beside the other, many trees filled with birds. But I no longer wanted to hear the birds calling and singing; I no longer wanted to see the trees, or the sky, or the light. Carefully

I closed the heavy wooden door. I began by making darkness all about me, feeling my way between the rows of wine barrels piled one on top of the other, to a certain place that I well knew. There was a heavy plank there that I used as a bench. I would sit on it, with my knees hunched, my elbows on my knees; and, blocking my eyes with the forefinger of each hand, my ears with the thumbs, and my nostrils with the two little fingers, I would try to imagine what "it could possibly be like"—that terrible thing that they had told us had to be, that impossible thing, death.

Why are little children not pious? Possibly because they are not afraid.

Little children are not "grateful" to God, or to anyone else. They find sufficient protection in their parents, and, as a matter of fact, it is the parents' natural function to provide this protection. Children feel safe. But, although they are not pious, they have nevertheless an extremely awakened metaphysical curiosity, and it is all the keener since they have not yet learned to be satisfied with the ready-made answers society holds in store for them. The great question for the metaphysician is also the great question for children. (They quash it soon enough because people make them ashamed to ask it.) Sooner or later they are compelled to see that there are questions one does not ask, and a feeling of embarrassment soon, and easily, overcomes their need to know. Yet, at first openly, and then secretly, they are prompted by a great curiosity (curiosity more than anything else) to investigate the essential problems, problems which, as adults, we all know perfectly well still assail us mightily, but which we refuse to recognize, because we have entrusted their solution to all sorts of authorities whom we judge to be infinitely more competent than we are ourselves.

What was it like after death?—yet all the while I kept telling myself that it was impossible that I should ever die. When I had pulled the barn door closed behind me, I remember what trouble I took to stop any sound from entering, or color or light; blocking my ears and eyes, trying hard not to see anything any more, or to hear anything any more, cutting myself off from taste or smell —since we were to be in a place where the senses no longer exist.

I tried not to think any more, saying to myself: "I am dead, I am still a little more dead." Only, at the back of my eyes, back of my closed eyelids, little flames would light up, colored fires, red, rose-colored, white, and then flashes of lightning.

I no longer saw outside myself, I saw inside my-self; I no longer heard the wind or the rain, or any sounds of the world outside, but all the clearer in the depths of my being I heard the secret rumblings in my body (the groaning vis-cera, the growling stomach, the blood pounding through the arteries).

I thought that I was stopping thought; but then I realized that I was only thinking that I was not thinking, having done no more than displace my thought, for how can thought be killed? I was still there, crouched on my oak plank, thumbs in ears, head in hands, invisible to others, but not invisible to myself: yet this sort of annihilation into which I was trying to force myself resulted in the very opposite—the excitement and exalta-tion of my inner being.

It was the season when they burned the heaped-up leaves of the chestnut trees, or those stems of wild clematis which are all pierced through with little channels that allow the smoke to circulate.

You try to see what it will be like "when we are dead," and all that you see is that you cannot die, or at least that death is something you cannot apprehend through the senses. You think you are smothering these senses in yourself, one after an-other; but all you are actually doing is to make them function in reverse. Possibly death, I said to myself, does nothing but make the senses function in reverse, and thus it becomes only another sort of life. And from there to telling myself that there is no death, or at least—since I alone could be the object of these reflections—that I myself would never die, was only a step and one soon taken.

Was this because I loved life? I still love life. Was it only through horror of death? I still have a horror of death. Was it not more likely that the closer we are to our origin, I mean to our birth, the sharper our premonition that there is something in us which is destined not to die? And we dare not speak of this for fear of ridicule. For it is a ridiculous idea and one which ceases to be ridiculous only when it is explained in some philosophical system, or in religious dogma; in other words, only after it has become thinkable—although it is actually unthinkable; only after it has found refuge in reason—even if by sleight of hand. For this idea is purely instinctive; it defies reason.

★

There is this passage in André Gide's "Journal": *"I know a man whom a single thought sufficed to plunge into deepest melancholy, the single thought that, in the near future, he would have to buy a new pair of shoes to replace those on his feet. This man's case should not be considered one of avarice; what he felt was a sort of distress at not being able to stand on anything lasting, definitive, absolute."* Here am I.

I do not feel any particular age. Physiologically, I am not aware that I have grown old. I can still wear the same clothes I wore twenty years ago. I do not think the way I walk has changed, or the pace at which I walk. I have remained supple and do not get out of breath. I talk to young men of twenty as though I were their contemporary, entirely unconscious of the fact that when they think of me they probably do not share my feeling about myself and doubtless see in my appearance something (a serious something) of which I cannot be aware.

I have lived withdrawn from the world, a fact which has allowed me to avoid certain disillusions common to men of my age. My contemporaries were attached to ideas which cruel events

have since invalidated. Therefore, they have
either given up belief in anything, or they cling
only to empty formulas, ideas which only their
official situation—for they belong to the generation now at the helm—permits them to endow
with a semblance of life. Never having followed
the fashions of the day, I do not happen to have
gone out of fashion. Never having been "in
chains," I do not now have to be freed. I have
never been, nor am I now, a Liberal, a Radical,
a Bourgeois, or a Capitalist. I stay in my own
little corner, with all the drawbacks that such a
position entails, but also with the advantages.
The advantages, today, are gradually becoming
clearer. For now we see those gentlemen who believed in the State (no doubt they still believe in
it) painfully witnessing the collapse of States all
around them; and those who believed in the stability of money now failing to understand why
they are ruined; and those who believed in an
arbitrary code of ethics (non-religious and compulsory) now contemplating with terror the recent perversions (or tyrannies) of this code of
ethics; and those who believed in "progress" now
having to learn that any kind of progress cuts
both ways, that this sword which they helped to
sharpen has finally turned its blade against them.

They never even dreamed that their realities might not be real. They had settled down in a relativism that was so comfortable, and so seemingly stable, that they had come to mistake it for an absolute. Now suddenly they perceive that circumstances alone, and accidental circumstances at that, had created a state of affairs from which they had profited, in the belief that it would last forever.

★

Our well-known ruling classes no longer rule anything. They are taken in by ideas over which they have no control, which come to them from the ends of the earth, which no longer submit humbly to their judgment, as books still do, but, on the contrary, predetermine that judgment by the advance publicity which automatically influences it. Yet even this would matter little, if, at the same time, most men did not lose the sense of their own value, their feeling for reality, hence their feeling for all measurement, and through that their feeling for proportion. We are now at the point where everything appears on the same plane—a plane where all sights and sounds from everywhere are intermingled: the weighty and the trivial, the tragic and the comic, the fugue and the hit-song—for the combination of screen, records and wireless makes it automatically possible to focus the public's attention upon a chosen object by a spotlight which plunges into deepest shadow whatever it has decided to ignore. Here is the final product of our much-touted "modern means of communication" that reach everyone from one end of the earth to the other. The public must accept this product and does accept it. The public no longer acts but is acted upon, no longer molds but is molded; it has become entirely passive in its uniformity. Fashions supplant each other swiftly. Everything parades by at a gallop. You are applauded and forthwith forgotten. No one has time to take hold of anything, to become attached to anything. No one has time to distinguish the essential from the inessential, the significant from the obviously insignificant; the seminal from the sterile; sycophantic imitation from true originality (with all its inherent slowness and difficulties). And the reward for originality comes much later, afterward. But now there is no *afterward*; we are under the régime of *news*—in which not the important, but the unimportant is featured: to wit, the daily press, which is interested only in items of the day, appeals only to the curiosity of the readers who keep it alive, makes great men of crooks, and murder a great event, and delegates the truly great things to the fringes of darkness, while the bright light is shed upon trivialities.

And Jesus is still born in the straw. Who could extract from the huge mass of facts and images continually piling up those of importance, I mean those which will take on importance in the future? Lenin worked for twenty years and no one mentioned him; it was only when he turned a whole part of the world upside down that his name was finally heard. What he was had never been remotely suspected by anyone; his achievement brought him to light. The bourgeois reading their newspaper are eternally fooled into accepting the newspaper's scale of values. In another domain, they ignored Rimbaud and still ignore Rimbaud; they ignored Cézanne and still ignore Cézanne; perhaps they know Einstein's name, but uniquely because of the grotesque aspect of a few images which the newspapers dug up from his doctrine, like that of the car traveling at the speed of light in which the passengers need never again sit up all night, or the famous image of the triangle, one side of which is bigger than the sum of the other two because the element of time has been introduced into the calculation of space. The seminal elements of life are never brought to our attention. Revolutions of all kinds are prepared in darkness—the political, the literary, and those in painting— and are therefore the more to be feared.

★

The position of the bourgeoisie has a tragic side because it is still linked to advantages once earned, perhaps, and deserved, but which are so no longer. For in their need to prove themselves worthy of their privileges they are driven to sudden bursts of activity, and this is the source of fascism. They are afraid, and this very fear gives them fresh energy and temporary reassurance. But their own ideology was revolutionary in the beginning and now they cannot prevent its logical consequence: another revolution, this time against themselves. For the French Revolution contained a whole series of revolutions only one of which materialized—the one made by the middle classes, the Third Estate, in successful reaction against the others. That was Thermidor. The revolutions which miscarried at the time will

now take place. The bourgeoisie will be responsible; they started the whole thing.

In man, an individual and a human being exist
side by side. The bourgeois is the person who has
lost all feeling for man's humanity and no
longer respects it; the person who, unable to perceive the humanity in man, sees only the individual—the individual as defined by his position in
society. He has the greatest esteem for those most
like himself, but a little above him. For in every
good bourgeois there is a feeling for rank and
promotion. The bourgeois hierarchy is like the
military hierarchy: you start out a private; if you
are lucky, you may end up a colonel.

The bourgeois is also the person who thinks
that money pays (the two definitions are not contradictory). In this respect many communists
are bourgeois. The bourgeois refuses to see that
money pays for time but does not pay man himself. For man's economic side is not everything.
Man can also be paid, and perhaps best paid, by
respect. I use the word "respect" cautiously for I
well know all the ambiguities it contains. But it
implies above all the idea of friendship, and man
has a special need of friendship. Let us say that

friendship touches the human being, while money touches the individual—always remembering that man is both an individual and a human being.

Man's inner being is unaffected by any other beings. And, since each human being is unique, essentially no man can be compared with any other. He is, therefore, indifferent to ideas of promotion or rank; yet, if he is not respected, he cannot live. But rank gives him no satisfaction whatever, even when he has to wear the insignia of a rank he never sought on the sleeve of his jacket, for rank concerns only the individual in man and sets him apart from others. There is in man something wholly independent. Yet our being, so entirely separate and aloof, needs to communicate with others, though on a different plane: we live through the love we give and receive. And respect is a form of love. The well-ordered state would take into equal account both the individual and the human being which, together, form man; in the well-ordered society authority would be modified by respect.

But bourgeois society has no respect for the human being. That is why it is a badly ordered society. Possibly all societies are badly ordered, differing only in the degree of imperfection. But there is this too: a badly ordered society may be a magnificently organized society; a society which is entirely contemptuous of the human being may perfectly well at the same time be most favorable to the development of the individual. It may have good roads, an efficient postal service, and a stable currency. Bourgeois societies have had all these excellent things and some still have them—wherein they are deceptively successful. What condemns these societies to an early disappearance is the revolt of the human being, the revolt of a great number of human beings, at present deprived of the respect which is their due; held in contempt, stifled, voiceless, without means of expressing themselves. But their revolt never reaches the political plane until they have suffered the extreme of poverty and hunger.

The all-important question is to know whether man is absolute or relative. The very concept of being involves the idea of the absolute. The human being cannot be classified nor can he therefore be identified with a class. I am not a communist. I am much less of a communist than the bourgeois who, having engendered communism, are horrified by it. It is their child, a parricidal child; its parents watch with terror as it finally turns against them. Among human beings, the thing that counts is nobility. To be human in the highest sense of the word, one must have a certain nobility—a nobility having nothing in common with the prerogatives of caste, nor yet with dogmas, nor yet with faith. I go further: the true human being requires a standard of measurements; he must have stature. But it is characteristic of the individual today that he no longer has stature.

For now, every day and in every way, the universe is more microscopically measured; but what standard of measurement remains that can be applied to man? The day has passed when man, because he was made in the image of God, still had a certain stature—or when gods were made in the image of man. But now where do we stand? What is our physical relation to the universe? What is our moral relation to a "whole," to a totality unaware of our existence and even unaware of its own? We must understand that the curtain is just rising on our tragedy; that we are facing the real crisis, of which the economic crisis is but a pale reflection. The tragedy is that man

no longer has a stature of his own, since he has
lost a common standard of measurement with the
material universe and, as a conscious being, has
no contact with a world in which he finds no consciousness. Because of his outer and inner dimensions, man's solitude is unequalled, for round
him nothing thinks or feels. Suddenly, man has
found himself exiled from the world.

I say suddenly because, although we have been
measuring things for a long time, it is only recently, through books, newspapers, schools and
compulsory education, that the results of these
measurements have begun to affect the masses.
The man who surveys the heavens with his telescope is relatively modern; still more modern is
the man who surveys the atom with his micro-
scope—for it proved equally necessary to mag-
nify both the firmament and the atom, the one
because distance makes it seem so small, the other
because it is indeed so small. A way had to be
found to bring both firmament and atom closer
before we could begin to grasp their reality, before we could feel their danger. They had to be
brought infinitely closer; in other words, the
quantitative relationship they bore to us, to our
human dimensions, had first to be emphasized.
Then the firmament and the atom were again re-

turned to the depths of their limbo, where they continue to live and ignore us, where each has assumed again its place in the universal scheme and those dimensions which overwhelm us.

For the moment, let me speak only of man's physical stature: in what does it consist? Has it lost all importance? Are we the only ones to see it, and if so, are we condemned to self-contemplation? For a long time only the scientists and the philosophers asked themselves this question. For a long time this question only appeared in books written by specialists for specialists. For a long time this self-questioning remained secret, and esoteric, and the answers formed a theory believed only by some. The whole question of our stature remained theoretical and only a few were concerned. Just lately, however, the concern has spread; I mean it has ceased to be a matter only for the few and affects the great majority. It is only very recently that the truth about our physical stature has begun to reach the masses: those who are at school, those who vote, who go to moving pictures, who read the newspapers, or even who do not read at all. But people in vast numbers, the masses, are not "objective." They are not interested in research for its own sake. Their only concern is for themselves. They do not think of a doctrine apart from its consequences, or pure speculation apart from life itself. They dramatize everything. They do not live in the mind alone, but in the stomach which may be empty, and in tired muscles, and in bodies shivering in the cold wind. The masses do not live by reason; they live by emotion. They ask: "What does it mean? What does it mean for us?"

Where indeed do we human beings belong in this scale of dimensions which has neither beginning nor end? We have, after all, a certain dimension of our own. It is infinitely small compared to the infinitely great spaces surrounding us, opening up all about us, and above and beneath us. Pascal was alone when he first uttered his cry of horror; today we are a hundred million, tomorrow there will be a billion, to utter the same cry. A hundred million men now suddenly feel themselves lost in space, just when they have lost their faith; or rather, to be exact, the realization of space has made them lose their faith. It is therefore as though they were twice lost, twice deprived of their human dimensions. We are now surrounded by a space impossible to measure at either of its extremities, and we have no standard of measurement great enough, or small enough, to enable us to fit ourselves in. Yet at both extremities, in the infinitely great firmament as in the infinitely small atom, the same proportion between the parts and the elements apparently persists forever, creating a strange symmetry which adds even more to the mind's confusion. For they tell us that there is not an atom, however microscopic, in which the mathematician does not discover the existence of other solar systems, containing the same spatial relationships between their component elements as those which allow the great planets themselves to gravitate. But in these limitless quantities, endlessly superimposed by increasing or decreasing masses, there is nothing to "touch the heart." The gods, for the pagan, were made to man's measure; while man, for the Christian, was made to the measure of God. But now there are no longer any gods. There is no room left for gods. We would not know what to do with them; they are useless. They are cast out by an ever-increasing knowledge of reality; what remains, perhaps, is God, by which I mean the Universe itself, by which I mean Totality. But measurement alone is incapable of distinguishing a person in that Totality, and therefore there is no other person in all the universe to give us our true measure. There is no one left but ourselves. Oh curious phenomenon! For the concept of "person" presupposes consciousness. Not only do we think, but we think of ourselves thinking. Not only do we feel, but we feel ourselves feeling. Not only do we act, but we judge ourselves in our action. Is there a God Who thinks as we think, is there a God Who feels as we feel and, if God acts, does He know that He acts?

God, for the Christian, was Supreme Consciousness, Perfection itself. The gods, for the pagan, not only had consciousness in common with man, but all his passions too. Man, therefore, used to have both a quantitative stature, since the universe was made to his measure, and a qualitative stature, since either he was made in the image of God, or he made the gods in his own image. But now the universe has become impersonal. The tragedy is that the universe now seems to us merely a monstrous assemblage of quantities, indifferent to themselves and to us. And this change has only just taken place within the last fifty or sixty years, a split second in the ages of our history. A relatively short time ago, man still had a roof over his head. But man's eyes, now informed by his brain that the roof is not made of firm, lasting material, will henceforth penetrate and

tear asunder this vault which once served to roof
his house, when the earth itself was his abode.
Now the house no longer has a roof nor has man
an abode. Even the earth itself is wholly lost, a
chance visitor in the spaces through which it wan-
ders while, little by little, it destroys itself. There
is no gainsaying that the scale is far too vast.
"How could such a scale as this consider me at
all?" man now asks himself. "How could I possibly attribute any importance to my own existence when the existence of the stars, even of the
greatest stars, is of so little consequence; when
there are actually billions of stars as great as our
sun, thousands of nebulae each containing as
many stars as there are in our Milky Way which
has become a mere pin-point in the vast emptiness through which it moves?" The disproportion
is too great.

Besides, man meets with nothing but silence
everywhere, and this silence frightens him. He
has knowledge of bodies everywhere, which have
no knowledge of him; he measures them, but
they do not measure him. "Ah, this is not a family. I live among strangers. I cannot even compare myself to them. For, to attempt a comparison, if I think of the atom, I become a monster,
although a relatively small one; if I think of the

60

stars, I become so completely shrunken that I can no longer see myself at all. There is nothing left but these quantities, and there is no longer any common scale. Or, I might better say, there is an infinitude of scales. I constantly move from one to another," man says to himself, "unless my work, my occupations or preoccupations, or a lack of imagination or too little sensitivity on my part, arbitrarily—and luckily for me—pin me down to a day-by-day dimension, made to order, in which both the universe of the stars and that of the atom are equally forgotten."

When the peasant of antiquity looked up over the hills in the rose-colored mists of morning and saw Venus, she was not much taller than the women of his village. When the storm came, it was Jupiter brandishing his lightning bolts, plainly visible on the horizon. Or he saw Vulcan hammering out his weapons at the forge. Or he saw Juno frowning. There was nothing in the gods that man could not immediately understand, since everything in them was but an extension of himself; since the deeds of the gods were human deeds, their passions human passions and, like the human beings above whom they dwelled, they, too, were inter-related and bound by family ties. They too, like human beings, were fathers and sons, husbands and wives; they too were jealous, passionate, envious, and full of hate.

How restful to the spirit to behold, on all sides, the gods in their fine, ordered dynasty—a sight one can still imagine today in our mountains, for the gods were conceived in the mountains and now it is in the mountains that they have taken refuge. It is still possible to greet them there once in a while as one goes by, with a little shock at feeling their presence again; not imprisoned in documents, nor buried deep in books, but still erect, wholly alive, plain to the naked eye. I remember that fine summer morning when we were driving along the edge of the Rhone toward the gates of the Valais. I wish I could describe the quality of the air that day, how limpid it was, how light, and again how dark. The light was strangely rose-colored and blue, as we passed from light into shadow. No one was about; everything was still. Two mountain ranges close together, one on the right, one on the left, with the bare rock magnificently carved as if to show every shape and possibility of sculpture, rose steeply three thousand meters from their broad, strong foundations, darker in color toward the foot because of the forests. But the bare rock was pink and yellow, gold and silver. You saw the peaks, then you no longer saw them, but you saw still others beyond. They were pyramids, they were columns, vanishing and reappearing, immense pillars, broad pediments, like those of a Greek temple, with overhanging cornices. And in this composition, endlessly disarranged and rearranged by the rapid advance of the car—high up, twenty-five hundred meters above us, resting on nothing, wholly aerial, held aloft by nothing, jutting out over the plain across tier upon tier of ravine and debris and snow-ice—a magnificent helmeted head leaned down a little toward us, filled with curiosity no doubt, filled with a desire to see us, to see human beings—with their inventions, their automobiles, their clothes made of English or Scottish cloth, their rugs and their coats. The plume on the helmet was of diamonds, the helmet itself bright metal; its golden face gazed straight at us, observing us, and it looked, as it crouched there watching us, like a chamois hunter lying in wait. "Look!" we said. But already it was gone. As the road changed direction, the mountain peaks changed too, one passing in front of the other, and already the one we had seen, eclipsed, was gone. It was then that Iris appeared, Iris, messenger of the gods. She came down to us in sudden, slanting flight through the air—so swift a flight that it tautened her veiled body from top of head to tip of toe. She, too, had come forth from the dead textbooks to re-enter life and, living, how gracefully she moved, at the same time imponderable and yet with body, of the earth and yet of the air, undefined and yet circumscribed, multi-colored, all the colors forever changing; and it was that straight line of her body at the center of the colors which alone gave direction, aim, and purpose to her flight. It was the sun itself, appearing to us through a narrow gap in the mountain range at our left, that sent us its light by this sudden delegation. Delegation is the word: the sun sent both messenger and message. "Make haste"; the word was spoken, and Iris hastened; an arrow grazed us and then we too had passed.

Mythology was born in the high mountains and it is to the mountains that we must return to re-live mythology.

And now the myths surrounded me. I had not gone there to seek them; they had sought me out. The car rolled smoothly on, but something else high above us was rolling too, rumbling down the mountainside, ever wilder, ever more barren and steep; and this something made the sound you hear when masons move heavy stones and the stones strike against each other; and thus I knew that the Titans, whom we can see no longer, were still busy at their prodigious tasks. Then the mountainside became vertical; it rose like a wall, and at that moment a thin watery mist drove against our faces and we heard a woman's laughter and many women laughing in reply. Our presence sent them into wild and precipitate retreat. They were the nymphs of the mountain torrent. We had startled them and now they hastened upward through the foaming waters toward the heights whence they had come. There they were; we could still see them. Laughing, they rose up through the falling waters; they clung to the waters with both arms and the moving waters moved their knees. They were there in great numbers, clad in white; some were higher, some closer to us; now they climbed swiftly, now they paused to turn their heads toward us. Again they climbed, helping one another, and then they paused once more. The wind caught their tunics and floated them out; the wind caught the ends of their tunics in misty foam. The nymphs, holding closely to the rocks, began to laugh again.

Already, alas, we were approaching a region inhabited by man, a region of houses, streets, shops and factories, whose tall chimneys belched out black smoke in dreary betrayal. The gods had vanished; yet, for a little while that morning, they had been with us. We had been in their own abode, in their high mountain realm where there is no sound but the sound they make, no motion but their own; where they are awe-inspiring, but approachable and friendly, glad to be alive, rejoicing in color; raised fantastically high above us and of heroic stature—yet not so immense, nor raised so high, as to escape the measure of man. They were greater than we; they were still our kind. Ephemeral and eternal, as we are, with arms and heads and legs like ours, with clothes covering their bodies, or else naked, but naked as we are. Venus is naked, Diana is clad. Venus is rose-colored, Diana is entirely white, and Iris is of every color. The nymphs wear white. And look, the one up there, the one so far up, so majestically enthroned, in her firmly pleated robes, pensive with chin on hand, dominating the entire assembly—that is Juno, mother of the gods.

Calm and peace are there; everything is pure; and above all there is security. There everything is clear and at the same time everything is alive.

In all our world there is nothing which is not composed of the same elements as we are, the outer elements and the inner, the form, feeling, attributes, temper, gesture or mood—they are all present everywhere. The gods are human; they have beards or are beardless; they laugh with our laughter; they have our voices, our tridents, our cloaks, our sceptres, our bows and arrows; our humor, our tears, our despairs and our joys. They live on the world's summits and their presence completes the world. They are found at the ends of the world and at its center. They command not only the earth and the waters but the air and the trees. They encompass all space which is made to their measure—but they are made to our own.

In Christian times, the peasant, looking up at the stars, saw God. What did it matter how immeasurably greater they were than himself, since God saw him, the peasant, and loved him, no matter how small he was? Not only did the peasant of Christian times see God with inner certainty, but God saw him. It was through his intelligence that he knew; it was through an intelligence—Intelligence itself—that he was known and, linking these two intelligences, there was the bond of love. It is impossible to imagine an immaterial God, impossible to form an image of an immaterial God, but it is entirely possible to love an immaterial God, once you know that He loves you. Since this God exists outside matter, since matter is wholly subservient to His will, the dimensions of matter lose all importance. Since spirit cannot be measured, how can the measurements we apply to matter affect it? The Christian was not appalled, as we are appalled, by the endless progression of numbers—since God, being infinite, is beyond any possible progression of numbers. And even this infinity of God does not frighten him, although he is unable to understand it, since he has been told that his own person is formed in the likeness of God and that God sent down to him His Son Who is, in One Person, both God and man.

How much more human even than pagan faith is this religion, how much better fitted to our measure, since God has been one of us, has once had exactly our dimensions, has once had a body exactly like our own; has lived not on the mountain tops, high above clouds, in the depths of the earth or in the heart of the forests, but on the contrary, as we do, in a house like one of ours, on a street like one of ours, eating and drinking, sleeping as we do, speaking to us; He was born and died, suffered and bled and cried out before He died—and yet was God. The only true difference between the pagan religion and the Christian lies in Christ's person, for from the moment that He exists, and that He is truly Christ, what can it matter about the vast abysses in which light moves straight ahead, taking hundreds and thousands and millions of years to reach us; in which the nebulae, like coiled snakes, uncoil and recoil themselves again without visible purpose; in which gases little by little increase in density, coagulate, liquefy and then from the liquid finally solidify, and at first are cold, then hot, and still hotter, and afterward appear to return again of their own volition toward their original consistency, toward their point of origin, which is the equalizing of temperatures, the progressive disappearance of hot and cold, a completely immobilized and lukewarm universe, the perfect symbol of death (from which nothing would ever be reborn)?

What then does it matter if our little earth and we ourselves, we men upon it, play a mechanical part in this fatal evolution? For here I must point out that the disaster is prodigious, and that it is not just a disaster to each one of us as persons, but also to all we have thought, all we have felt, all we have made, to all our achievements, to all our masterpieces, all our paintings, all our sculpture, and not only to our palaces, but to our simple homes; to all our inventions, to all our machines, to all that justifies our existence, to everything in which we take pride. I must point out that everything shall pass, that we ourselves shall pass—along with the memory of our having lived. . . . The foundations of everything shall pass, by which I mean the earth, and our sun, and our solar system, returned at the last to a pale gaseous substance without consciousness or memory, suspended, lukewarm, conscious of nothing, not even of itself, somewhere in the infinite.

But what does all this matter, says the Christian, since Christ exists and is Spirit and I myself am spirit too; since through the spirit I can reach Him, and through Him reach God, for He is both man and God and since, after all, I was conceived in God's likeness, and the presence of Christ in our midst is formal proof of this fact? What matters the destruction of the universe, for it is but a material universe; what matters the disappearance of earthly life, of that which we call life, since the earth is not its true abode, and life on earth is only false life, says the Christian; a wholly provisional life, a life of trial and waiting after which true life will come? We are born for eternal life, says the Christian, so how can the finite moment matter? And what do we care about the false quantities which obsess us since, being but quantities, they are entirely illusory? We have taken our whole refuge in quality, which means love, because God loves us and He is perfect love. He is perfection in all things and He frees us from the imperfection of numbers, distances, measurements, which may possibly mean something to the mind, but not to the heart. The heart—the heart is at peace; the heart listens and loves. It is thus that the Christian is able to hold his stature in the midst of the upheaval which technical progress has brought to the universe. The Christian can still hold his stature because he is not part of the universe, or rather, because he is part of it only through his body—which he has surrendered from the start. The Christian can still hold his stature by grappling to himself, at the moment of shipwreck, a precious certitude— which neither the shifting gales nor the crashing waves can tear from his grasp.

71

The heavens we see and the heavens we do not see are filled with innumerable stars circling round and round. What does it mean? Does it mean anything? The planets turn round the sun, the sun turns round something else, that something else turns round still something else, and all this makes our Milky Way; yet even the Milky Way is nothing at all because it, too, revolves round something greater than itself. I am a human being. What is my stature? What is man's stature? Is greatness nothing more than the piling up and clustering of cells? If so, we are nothing at all. But, on the other hand, if greatness can be split into fragments, into the infinitely minute atom, yet still remain greatness—what then? If so, again we are nothing at all. Or does greatness lie in a certain quality in no way akin to quantity, having no dimensions in common with quantity—though housed in it?

We remember Pascal's saying: "Even if the universe were to crush him, man would still be nobler than what kills him because man knows that he dies; but of its advantage over him the universe itself is unaware." Man knows, and he knows that he knows. Therein lies his greatness.

But greatness exists only when it is recognized, recognized by someone else. Is there then someone outside of man who can perceive man's greatness? For man vanishes, and his works also vanish. Indeed, this is his only certainty.

Man has never been so exposed to the universe as today. Even when he quietly minds his own business in his corner, the universe intrudes upon him. The world around him is in continual and ever more rapid motion; it is as though the world, all of the world, were constantly present at every point everywhere in the world—the automobile, the airplane, the radio; images, sounds, voices. Man is no longer called upon to act; he has only to let himself be acted upon. And the outer reality which assails him is richer than his wildest dreams. Meanwhile, however, he feels himself becoming smaller and smaller—precisely because of his own passivity. He grows increasingly passive while external reality becomes increasingly active. His own actions no longer proceed from within him, no longer take effect outside him; no longer does man, by his domination of matter, impose his own dimensions on the living world. Rather it is matter and objects which impose their dimensions on man, and, confronted by their immensity, he disappears. They overwhelm him; they reduce him to despair. Man has been robbed of his custom of giving the gods a human form. For a long time he lived by it; unconsciously, it was his consolation. And now, from every direction the universe breaks upon him wave after wave, and the towering waves appall him. Now he is told that at long last the time has come when he will know the secrets of the universe—but will this knowledge suffice? He is told that the universe is his to command, at least partially—but is partially enough? Only the complete subservience of the universe to his will would be enough and he sees that this is unattainable. He knows perfectly well that by mastering one new force, he frees others of which he did not even dream, although it would perhaps be more accurate to say that the forces free themselves, for they existed already, though their origins and effects were unknown.

At the same time man sees that the forces he has succeeded in harnessing have an equal capacity for what he calls good and for what he calls evil; that they are as capable, depending on the circumstances, of destroying as of creating, of killing as of curing, since they are indifferent both to evil and to good. But man is not indifferent. How then is man even to curb them, let alone make them go where he wants? For he cannot guide them without an idea of where he is going himself—but what if he no longer knows? Or what if he doubts the ideas he still has? Yet, if he looks back for guidance to what he has built in the past, which, after all, represents a positive achievement, he begins to doubt even that, for he sees that all he created is ephemeral and then, because he lacks a scale, he no longer sees the greatness with which he thought he had endowed his work. For you cannot measure greatness by the yard.

And so, once again, what is greatness? Does it actually exist, or was it only an illusion of the ancients, who thought themselves great because the world was small? Today, man is assailed by the greatness which can be measured: the speed of a plane, the speed of the stars, the speed of light. Man is assailed both by the greatness which he himself has originated and by the greatness over which he has no control. Man is beginning to believe only in measurable and therefore demonstrable greatness; he is unable to recognize the other, the spiritual kinds, for they are precisely the kinds which cannot be proved experimentally, but must be experienced. Man no longer trusts his inner experience; he weighs the atom and the stars. Man has ceased to be an artist; he has become a scientist. Science proceeds cumulatively by accretion, whereas art takes shape from within; science proceeds through calculations, and the results obtained are apparent, whereas art contents itself with the attempt to quicken and only thus to convince. A tunnel ten miles long is impressive—but what of a building such as the Louvre? Here are two orders of greatness. For a tunnel twenty miles long would be still more impressive—but what of a building twice as big as the Louvre? In its day the Eiffel Tower was impressive: it is three hundred meters high; you can see that. But in a painting by Rembrandt there is no greatness at all unless you believe it to be there. The two greatnesses have nothing in common. Yet we use the same word for both. Why?

Men sometimes get the impression of greatness from the material, sometimes from the spiritual. In both cases the impression is the same, and it is emotional. Does the word greatness allude to anything beyond these successive impressions? If not, the concept of greatness would be purely an æsthetic concept; it would only describe the beautiful, and how beauty moves man no matter what its origins—and as we have just seen, its origins are twofold. But we should note that after man has been moved by beauty, he questions himself, and finds that one kind of beauty exalts him lastingly, whereas the other kind crushes him, since he has no common measure with it. Furthermore, he finds that crushing beauty forces itself on him as reality, whereas beauty that exalts does no more than beg his consent, which he is free to grant or to refuse. The first kind needs only the help of calculating machines and reason, but the second, on the contrary, hostile to every sort of calculation, needs only emotion and belief. . . .

★

Material greatness is wholly relative. Man's actual size still has some meaning when compared to that of a kitten; it no longer has any meaning at all (at least no useful meaning) when—to choose a dimension which, though vast, can yet be accurately gauged—we compare it to the distance that separates us from the nearest star. For here we are cast into the terrifying abyss where numbers progress in both directions toward that total absence of finality which we call the infinite and in relation to which the greatest as well as the smallest numbers lose all significance.

That is why man has had to break down the world of material greatness into compartments, fitting one on top of the other, and thus, within each of these subdivisions, establishing for his own convenience proportions by which greatness can not only be measured but also visualized, thereby becoming specifically human. For man has a certain power to impose his will on space; he has a certain power over material greatness. But has he any such power over the other greatness, the spiritual? Space and matter tend to shrink in direct proportion to man's increasing powers. For instance, the distance covered in one hour by an engine is constantly increasing. The distance itself, of course, remains unchanged; what changes is the obstacle it opposes to man's will. From this man draws certain conclusions as to his own stature (although that is of a different order) because he sees that here, at least, he can overcome material greatness by virtue of that other greatness which is his spirit.

Man is not just an artisan, he does not simply make things; he thinks and feels before he makes things. Because of this, there are works of his which, while they are not great materially speaking, are nevertheless recognized as great by everyone: a painting, for instance, perhaps a very small painting, or a poem, or a statue, or a church. Thus man establishes a connection in his mind, despite the innate difference, between greatness that can be seen and greatness that cannot be seen; between greatness that is measurable, and greatness that is felt.

When do we say that a particular act is a great act? To what extent is such action necessarily material? Action can have material consequences; but its source is not material. Joan of Arc's ridding France of the English is an example of greatness in action and it is quite true that her act resulted in a tangible greatness; yet even this greatness is not measurable—at least not at its source. It is obvious that Napoleon ended by turning Europe upside down, but the original cause of that upheaval was first lodged in a human brain, where it had no dimensions. There is the greatness of things and there is the greatness of man. There is the grandeur of Saint Francis of Assisi; but there is also the secret grandeur of the man who is humbly devoted to his task; who acts out of devotion to an image which surpasses him, and in so doing increases his own stature. For spiritual greatness means the development of that part of our being which thinks and feels.

And perhaps it is here that the two orders of greatness can meet and be reconciled—though it is well to bear in mind that even spiritual greatness can descend to material possessiveness, and that some men and nations are not satisfied simply to exist but also seek to possess. Finally, then, there are different kinds of greatness—the lasting and the perishable—and so it is essential to recognize the roots of the different kinds, for some consist in a false animation, impressive for the moment, but which only distracts man and amuses him, while others are rooted in profound possibilities of improvement which man perceives in himself and which need only be developed.

What is greatness in a nation if it is not both spiritual and material? For it is in the people as a whole that the two orders of greatness can be reconciled. Greatness in a people consists in the fusion of different kinds of greatness, and to this is added a special collective greatness which is more than the sum total of its elements.

Peoples, like individuals, form an idea of themselves beyond what they really are, and it is toward the realization of this idea that they move. There can be no real development if they are only marking time, although the stir they make may be considerable and for a time misleading; they are at a standstill unless they have a purpose, a goal. But in the end nothing is gained if nothing is expressed, if what is achieved remains untold, for achievement is a form of greatness, but the recording of achievement is another form of greatness.

Here is where the poet comes into his own.

Take even Queen Elizabeth's reign: what would it have been without Shakespeare? For Shakespeare appeared, and of the two he is the greater. Marathon and Salamis, what would they be, had they merely been fought and never sung? For there also exists that greatness which is the greatness of telling, the greatness of expression: we have only to remember the Greeks we learned about in school and how small their country was.

We measure a nation in size against the nations surrounding it and we say that it is a small nation; we measure a nation's true significance against that of the nations surrounding it and we call it great. Countries, whose importance is measured only by the space they occupy, disappear, and in the end it is as though they had never existed; countries which have expressed themselves survive their fall because they are established in man's memory, and have there acquired another

81

sort of life—a life which is, strictly speaking, limitless. The act counts less than the echo produced by the act. And here is where expression comes in—expression which is poetry, whether in words, color, line, volume or sound. For the truth is that, if it is the act alone which counts at the moment, what is said about the act determines its future. The act, if you like, belongs to history, and is passive in the face of history; but what is said of the act creates its own legend by which it goes on living in a continual, everlasting action of its own.

At the moment, it is the act which dominates; at the moment, the political takes precedence over the poetic; thus there is a conflict between the two orders of greatness. Or we can put it this way: there is a conflict of values because one kind of greatness, that of action, obvious and advantageous, brings more immediate returns; whereas the other greatness, the kind which gives expression to action, is a long-term investment. Still there is conflict, because action is never unaware of expression and, knowing the power latent in expression, envies it. There is unceasing rivalry between the political and the poetic, which are two separate orders of greatness. Action fears opinion, for action well knows that it depends on opinion. Yet action possesses the means to stifle opinion constantly, not even deliberately, but simply because action breeds action and is therefore convincing; because a succession of acts, infinitely diversified, is always fertile in sudden drama; and also because most men are only interested in action and can see nothing beyond the act—and thus action fills the stage. The result of all this (let us repeat) is that great things must be born in obscurity, for great things are those which can only find expression later. Though a rich future is in store for them, they are infinitely poor at birth. Their greatness is still potential, embryonic. Great things are silent at the start, held in reserve for their future task, and do not intrude or reveal themselves.

The day comes at last when the captain departs, when there is no longer a Duce or Fuehrer: it is then that the poet, whom for so long they silenced, can be heard. The poet's voice rises in the new stillness, for now all the others have been silenced. It may even be that the poet is dead, yet his presence is felt. It is then, indeed, that the poet really emerges; it is then that expression supplants action and effaces it. For all things vanish, but that which is expressed takes longer to disappear.

★

It is not happiness that man seeks; his need is for plenitude. What must be determined, therefore, is whether complete fulfillment is possible without first extending the meaning of life from an immediate to a more general significance. In other words, can there be fulfillment without an absolute?

You would have to find something to take the place of God. Up till now there has been only one absolute: God, or the idea of God.

Mind, emotion, body: man has many parts, and these parts are separate. Man is discontinuous in a discontinuous world. It is God who, till now, has brought continuity to man and to the world.

Man is doubtless capable of knowing plenitude without God, but this knowledge he only captures intermittently, reaching up to grasp it and then falling back again. But the essential characteristic of plenitude is that it must be lasting; and it was God, it was the Absolute, who made plenitude continuous, who made man safe against the vicissitudes of change.

With the existence of God everything is clear, for we see that God fills all the empty spaces and it is from emptiness that we suffer. Perhaps the idea of God occurs to man's mind only because there are empty spaces in him. Man does not know; man is a void. But what is it that man does not know? He does not know *everything*. It is only by knowing *everything* that he can fill his emptiness. In God, man knew everything.

Man never has what he wants, because what he wants is *everything*. It was only in God that he could have everything. Man suffered in the flesh and, because his suffering served no useful purpose, he did not know why he suffered; but perhaps the suffering was not useless when related to God, when related to the whole. That is why the idea of God allowed him to feel fulfillment in suffering, for it is possible to have plenitude, even in suffering.

Man's happiness comes from partial success. For a time, the man in love knows what it is to be happy. The schoolboy who has just passed his examinations is happy for a time. The business man who has had a success is happy for a time. It is as though happiness were only the harmonious prolonging of a happy experience which temporarily prevents our hearing the discords within us. Some happy incident fills us and momentarily conceals the parts within us which it does not touch; but gradually it dissolves and, dissolving, reveals them again. Once more the empty spaces are laid bare; perhaps after all everything is emptiness, and that is the thought which we cannot endure.

There are moments, perhaps, when man feels a complete fulfillment here and now, but they are extremely rare. There are moments, perhaps, when everything is "all right"—without God. Humanism substitutes the idea of usefulness to society for that of God, but this involves a total transformation of society and, as a first requisite, it requires one to believe in a new society. But I am talking about the world as it still exists today and I cannot avoid seeing that in this world things are never entirely "all right" and that the moments when happiness and success combine to make possible the illusion of fulfillment are always brief and fleeting.

My needs, while various, are relatively few. My health must be good and my family's health must be good. My work must be going well. My house must be in order. My clothes must be clean and I must have money enough not to have to think of it. There must be a blue sky and sunlight, and not only must I be happy myself but those close to me must also be happy. And, above all, I must have all these things at the same time. Yet they are never present at the same time. They are never there simultaneously; they can only be there one after the other. But the idea of plenitude presupposes that everything comes together at the same time. For plenitude does not consist in the presence of many of the parts: it is the sum of all the parts. That is why an earthly plenitude is always fleeting; for everything in this world is in motion and that motion leads to death.

Humanism, having adopted the hypothesis that God is a lie, will be compelled to overturn everything in the world. For, after all, our whole world was built on the idea of God. Even a people like the Chinese, for whom the idea of God is a vague idea, still keeps it alive in its subconscious. In humanism, however, nothing exists but man. Humanism can only promise us plenitude in a society which embodies all humanity. It can only promise plenitude to the individual through participation in all humanity's lordship over nature, each man's share being determined by his capacity and circumstances. The old religions offered us God, or the demi-gods, or else the Man-God; humanism offers us mankind and nothing more—but a mankind destined to become God.

In serving humanity man serves himself, but humanity is continually advancing. Man adds his own motion to humanity's. But if man and humanity were to move in different directions, their efforts would be contradictory and destroy each other. Consequently man must move only in a given direction so that every advance he makes adds something to what already exists: hence the idea of progress. There is always something ahead of us and we must catch up with it, and just as we catch up, it goes ahead again, for this is a race which has no end, but it is also a race which exalts us. Man will find fulfillment only through complete self-sacrifice for the progress of humanity, as it is only through the advance of all humanity that he himself can advance, his own progress being of no importance unless it contributes to the progress of humanity as a whole.

Hence the notion of heroism. Heroism means the sacrifice of self to a cause, to any one of a number of causes: the soldier's heroism which is the sacrifice of self to country; or the poet's heroism which is the sacrifice of self to poetry; or the Christian's heroism which is the sacrifice of self to God. And now there is, or there will be, another heroism: the sacrifice of self to one's fellow man; the sacrifice of man, the individual, to collective humanity. There are, for instance, these young Soviet girls falling through space with their parachutes, and they are exactly like the Christian virgins who went to meet the lions in the arena. What the virgins did in the name of God, the Soviet girls do in the name of humanity. Their God is man—deified in his progress; not deified as he is, but as he should be—and they make sacrifices to enable him to become what he is to be.

★

Nothing truly great can be accomplished without faith. The Soviets show this clearly enough; the Soviets have a faith.

Man has stature only so long as he can still believe in himself; but belief in himself is possible only when he believes that there is something that surpasses him, yet at the same time presupposes his existence.

Man needs to believe that he is indispensable. Man needs to be convinced not only that he exists, but that he will never cease to exist. For man is little or nothing in space, though it is possible that he may have importance in time, and therefore he sees quite well that when he thinks of himself only in terms of space, he is destroying one part of his twofold nature. Man sees that his meaning lies in eternity: "For I love you, I too, oh eternity," said Nietzsche. And there are three ways of conceiving eternity: the Christian way, which sees eternity in God; the materialist (or Soviet) way, which is the concentration of the whole individual upon the instant; and finally the philosophical way, which is the infinite succession of instants, each ephemeral in itself, inevitably reborn.

One must end by recognizing that it is only possible to love in eternity. That is why one must take care to act in all things as though one were to last forever.

★

May I be forgiven my clumsy insistence on a few elementary truths, for I know only too well that it is considered bad form to spend time on them—especially when one purports to be a writer. The cultivated man may of course debate them in private, against his better judgment and because he is forced to do so; but he will take great care not to discuss them in public. For since the questions they raise are unanswerable, at least by reason, it is childish to ask them. They can lead only to poetic effusion and moreover to a poetry that is worn pretty thin: the poetry of *why,* to which no doubt we ought to prefer the science of *how.*

Yet are not these precisely the questions which interest all men and I mean the nameless men who do not argue, but live, suffer and feel? Let us leave specialization to the specialists: they work at the tips of the branches; but these questions are like the trunk of a tree, rough-fibered and hard. The fact that an epoch such as ours should question the validity of accepted beliefs can only mean that it has weighed all the old metaphysical and religious solutions, has even accepted them again for a time, and has then rejected them. And what does this mean, if not that our very rejection now drives us toward revolutionary solutions—revolutionary because the society we know was founded on definite metaphysical and religious principles? The real crisis is a metaphysical crisis; the economic crisis is secondary because it is physical. For, consciously or unconsciously, man first asks: "Who am I?" and only later asks: "What do I possess?" The Christian, by possessing nothing, possessed everything. But what happens when man is no longer Christian? Are we not in the presence of a phenome-

non born of the despair with which man has
looked upon his fate and the fate of the world,
and of man's need for compensation? Man no
longer knows what he is, so he seeks to possess.
He now applies to himself the same quantitative
criteria which he has applied to the universe. He
sees, for instance, that he is hungry while others
eat their fill; that he has no room to himself
while others live in palaces; that his clothes are
old and shabby while others wear new clothes.
The man who owns nothing—that is, the majority of men—the man who has been taught to
evaluate in nature only what can be counted
(one man, ten men, a million men), has become
a mere quantity. He bases his claims on the fact
that he represents a number and a quantity.
Therefore he finds himself facing a world in
which mankind is divided—he cannot help observing—into a small number of men who exploit and a large number of men who are exploited. If the only question is to *have*, it is impossible for him not to notice that a few people
have and most people have not.

Here again the bourgeois or the capitalists are
responsible. For it was the bourgeois who first
made up their minds to have, to have as much as
possible. It was the bourgeois who first saw man

as a mere quantity to be put to use and who said: "How can we make it pay?" And so it is not entirely unnatural that man, who for so long has been used as a source of profit, should finally ask himself how he can put an end to exploitation, especially at a time when people have succeeded in convincing him that he has only one life to live, that there is no other life of any kind anywhere, that this short life soon ends and that if it comes to an end there can be nothing afterwards—and especially no kind of Judgment Day, no sentence, and no redress either, so that justice is something belonging entirely to this world, something to be settled here and now, or nowhere and never. It is therefore not enough to say that the Soviets have all sorts of excuses for condemning religion; it is not enough just to say that they are bound to suppress it since they must obviously suppress forces hostile to themselves; let us rather say that the Soviets are morally obliged to condemn and suppress religion in the name of the faith by which they live. Why accuse them of fanaticism? There is always fanaticism wherever there is active faith.

The bourgeois, too, is often an atheist, but a passive one. He does not believe strongly enough in his atheism to make it a principle of action.

His atheism remains passive, whereas Soviet atheism goes into action, for it is an anti-faith, in other words another kind of faith (and therein lies its superiority). Bourgeois atheism is based on tolerance; it is perfectly willing to exist at the side of faiths that contradict and oppose it; it says, "I do not believe, but I do not prevent you from believing." The bourgeois does not even believe strongly enough that he does not believe. For every religion or anti-religion projects the consequences of its principles into infinity; therefore, bourgeois tolerance finally results in nothing but confusion.

At the present time bourgeois society is in a state of extreme confusion. A part of it believes that God exists; for the rest, God does not exist. The foundation of all ethics and indeed of any possible sociology is sometimes denied, sometimes affirmed, but most of the time is deliberately ignored. Bourgeois society today is an incoherent aggregate of individuals only saved from total collapse by an extremely complicated armature of law—not to mention armies, police, courthouses, custom houses, and monetary systems. It may be—and this is a more profound reason—that what still holds it up, though very precariously and only for a short time, is its rooted indifference, the total incapacity of most of its members to make up their minds to choose and therefore to love and therefore to hate. In consequence, aware of the physical dangers that they would incur were the system to collapse, they still prefer to make the best of it, to hold on to it, despite its drawbacks. It is a society, crystallized on the outside, but containing the elements of decomposition. In other words, it is no longer a society in the real sense of the word; rather, it is several societies all living together, all hostile to each other—though mostly unaware of the fact; societies in which no one believes that his personal faith should mean anything to anyone else—a weak manner of believing, for he who believes strongly, believes in a truth which is not only true for himself but for everyone. The bourgeois atheist says: "God is absurd"; he does not say: "God is an evil"; or, if he says so, he does not see, or refuses to see, the inevitable consequences of that evil and does nothing to fight them.

Communism is the first example (at least in modern times) of an attempt to found a society entirely on a single plane: that of the visible material world. The communists are trying for the first time to create a social order in which God is not only forgotten but said not to exist. This is the aspect of communism which particularly interests us because it reveals the difference between communist society and our own. For anyone can see that we—I mean the nations of the West—pay little heed to God. The Soviets, on the other hand, pay great heed to Him. They fight Him, they even fight His absence; in other words, they fight Him by fighting those who still believe in Him, and thus, in a way, keep Him alive. For Soviet atheists do not simply say: "God does not exist." They say: "We must destroy even the concept of the existence of God, for it is on this concept that human injustice is based." They speak for all the exploited peoples of the world and they say: "There is only one God; the God of those who exploit you." All they are evoking is a phantom, but the strange thing is that in evoking it they bring the phantom back to life, they bring God back to life, so that God becomes far more alive in their minds—although only as a phantom and a lie—than He is in ours. For they act and plan *against* Him, while we act and plan and behave as though we had forgotten His existence. They draw from Him, I mean from the very act of denying Him, a fundamental stimulus which stirs them emotionally and therefore moves them to act; in other words, without their knowing it, all their acts are determined by this basic denial. Their ethics, for instance, although meticulously anti-Christian, completely the reverse of Christian, make a wonderfully symmetrical parody of Christian morality, or rather of Christian moralizing. For they, too, are busy "reforming" drunkards or "reclaiming" those who have strayed from the path of virtue—not for the sake of God, however, but for the sake of society. Society replaces God. You must have faith in society as you had faith in God. Atheism becomes a faith; it too believes in a "better world." The atheist, that kind of atheist, has his own (theological) hope, and later on we shall see what it is. This atheism, by the complete reversal of all metaphysical values, is building an entirely new world and, indeed, that is the only way to build an entirely new world. It is giving man once more a stature—where he had lost all stature. It no longer sees man made in the image of God; it no longer places him, as did the pagans, in a finite world made to his measure. It rejects the supernatural, denying even the possibility that there can be a supernatural; it rejects the fear and awe

97

of the natural extending into limitless space. But at least this atheism attempts to give man a just and proper place in human society.

Again, these questions: What is man? Where does he come from? Where is he going? Here they are again, always these same questions which are absurd, of course, and we know that they are absurd, but that is why we ask them. We envy the minds in which they do not arise—delicate, sophisticated, cultivated, trained in all the subtleties of analysis, but with one failing: they approach a problem, all problems, from the outer edge—if you can put it that way. They are the minds which the Ecole Normale produces every year, and the Sorbonne too, and Centrale, and Polytechnique, and all the other universities— minds which are doubtless very diverse, but have one common trait: a strange fear of radicalism, in other words, an eternal refusal to dig down to the roots. The Soviet mind is more crude—and for this I prefer it. The communists are more brutal, but therefore more human. The communists, as we have seen often enough, are not afraid of being ridiculous; whereas specialists in every field fear being ridiculous beyond anything else, and that is why they take refuge in specialization. Meanwhile the world falters on. The world stumbles along as best it can, and the specialists leave it alone, for they say they are incompetent outside the limits of their own specialization. But the Soviets intend to remake the world.

You can say at least this for the communists: they have seen men suffer and, having seen men suffer, they want to put an end to suffering. I know, of course, that they have recognized only one kind of suffering. Nevertheless, their first effort is an attempt to eliminate physical suffering in this world—the physical suffering of being hungry, and badly housed, and ill-clad; at least they get down to the case of man, and of man as he is most often, and they intend to remake the world—and that is a kind of greatness.

The philosophers, the moralists, the sociologists, those subtle and delicate spirits we have mentioned—they may perhaps have a passion for abstract humanity; but have they ever had a passion for man himself? If they felt this passion for man himself, would they still refuse (because of their scruples, their integrity, as they call it), would they still refuse to ask themselves what the ordinary man is always asking: "What am I, what am I doing here on earth?" For the ordinary man is essentially a metaphysician, although he does not know it. Confusedly, he seeks an explanation for what he feels. Hungry, he asks himself: "Who is to blame for my hunger?"; lonely or sad: "Why is it that I am alone and sad?" Dimly, he gropes for the why, and the why of the why.

Lying stretched out beneath a tree, or sitting on the bank at the edge of the highway with their arms round their knees and their heads bowed, what in the world are they thinking about—those old farmhands out of work, the men whom I see every day as I pass? And those other men with bundles on their backs whom I meet on winter nights near the town hall and who stop me to ask the way to the police station? For we still have an old custom in our country which recognizes the right of these people, every two months—for two nights running, if I am not mistaken—to a free bowl of soup and a mattress, enough to appease their hunger and to let them sleep their fill; they have this right provided their papers are in order, and all they need do is to apply at the police station. They ask me: "Where is it?",

100

raising a finger to a hat which is usually frayed and old, as they too are usually frayed and old, having reached the age when day by day their strength fails them a little more. Their strength was their only capital; it goes on shrinking. They have only the interest on the capital, the interest which is daily dwindling and will soon be zero, as they undoubtedly have to admit to themselves when night falls and the wind blows and it rains and they are out on the slippery, muddy roads, and they walk alone, wearing their only suit (their work clothes are in the bundle on their backs) and carrying some tool, such as a scythe with the haft removed.

What in the world can they be thinking about? And who will answer their questions? They are old men, men of fifty or sixty (not so old after all); but they are men without hope.

Articulate people who express themselves aloud, the articulate few who write and can thereby demonstrate that they exist and have opinions, these people are guilty of having divided humanity into two parts; and because they have the luxury of leisure, they concentrate upon that small part of humanity which also has the luxury of leisure. But the communists concentrate upon that part of humanity which has no leisure at all. The articulate few have turned their backs—out of good manners and social conventionality, somewhat as though they were in a parlor—on questions which they do not need to ask, on those very questions which people without leisure are compelled to ask. But the communists ask these necessary questions. The articulate few have been far too indulgent and considerate of bourgeois thinking—and by "bourgeois" I mean people with incomes, living in security, who never have to ask themselves whether society is badly organized since they owe their security to the way it is organized; who never have to ask themselves whether injustice in that society is not the rule rather than the exception, since they have the best of reasons for not thinking that society is unjust.

Philosophers and sociologists have unwittingly divided humanity; for them, there is only a small number of men whom they consider qualified to deal with certain subjects: subjects, among others, such as metaphysics and sociology. The philosophers and sociologists do not see that there are many men who, while they perhaps do not study these questions, are *living* them, for these questions lie at the very roots of their threatened existence—a man who is hungry, a man who is cold, a man who is without friendship, without love, without a hearth, without clothes to wear, or without shelter. All such men may well ask: "Why?" And the answer vouchsafed them, if any, is: "You are to blame," and they are told no more.

But the man whose thoughts we do not know (the one who asked me the way to the police station) lies stretched out on an army bed in a room with a locked door and barred windows. He is rolled up in an old army blanket; he is warmed all through his body (it is doubtless this wholly unaccustomed warmth which keeps him from sleeping) and his thoughts go round and round. Ah, he keeps turning over, way in the back of his mind, old thoughts, and—what is so wonderful—he does not express himself aloud (how wonderful this is); he expresses himself only by a sigh, or a hand closing and a clenched fist—but clenched at whom or at what? He is not able to "speak"; though those others are only too well able to "speak," and today only those who speak are counted, on public platforms, in parliaments, in courts, in political meetings, in the daily press. There are all those talkers, and then there is the man who is silent; all those who proffer and profess second-hand ideas—lawyers, officials, journalists; and then the man who, if he could speak, would only express ideas which he has actually lived—but those ideas are so hard to express, and anyway it would do no good to express them.

Communism is not interested in sensitivity, distinction, or tact. Communism has faced all the rudimentary human questions. It has dared to go to the roots of these questions: therein lies its strength. It has not even shown respect for the achievements of the society it has undertaken to destroy, for it attacks all society, saying: "So much the worse for society; so much the worse for what is good in society." Communism was and is convinced (and perhaps it is right) that you cannot reconstruct a society (as it most certainly wants to do) except upon the ruins of the existing society or régime; that you cannot start building, until you have razed to the ground the whole ancient edifice and even dug up the ground itself —for communism attacks the very foundations of society. Communism claims that this is for the sake of justice; it assumes that the social order in which we are still living is based on injustice, and therefore attacks the substructure on which this order rests, for thus the whole of society can be brought crashing down. Unlike "social democracy," communism is intolerant of a "composite" style; it is not reformist—and here again it shows greatness. The communist ambition is to achieve a "pure" style, in other words, an original style.

But here we must take care to point out that the answers of communism to the various essential and elementary questions asked by humanity are exclusively in terms of social order. The questions which the man lying on the cot in the police station keeps asking himself—though confused, they are still on the level of metaphysics—are transposed by communism and brought down to the level of this physical world of matter. For communism thinks that there is no other level. When faced with the existence of certain kinds of suffering, communism does not say—and would be horrified to say: "Human nature is to blame"; communism says: "Society is to blame." For the communist, fundamentally, is a man who does not believe in original sin. When I say this I do not mean that it is simply the dogma of original sin which he rejects, for that is obvious; the communist even rejects the idea of original sin considered as a pure hypothesis. He not only completely refuses to accept the idea of man's fall or his dethronement. He goes further; he does not even admit that man's powers are subject to certain limitations—and here we are already entirely outside the realm of pure theology. For one does not have to be a theologian to know, from experience, that man probably never acquires anything without simultaneously losing something else as a direct result of his achievement and that to believe, for instance, that all technical progress implies a gain for man, shows a wholly false conception of man's real nature. For instance, it is not at all certain that man gains anything by being able to move faster, and it might be easy to show that the very fact that everyone now moves faster tends to re-establish all the complications from which man thought that modern transportation would free him— for everything is relative. Also, it might not be very difficult to prove that the more man masters what must be called his secondary powers, those of a mechanical nature, the more he loses control of his primary powers, those of an intuitive nature, which are now steadily withering away.

Communism, however, refuses to concede this. Communism is not discouraged by defeats or delays or reverses; it considers them temporary. Communism has faith in man. It is the communist view that man's powers are global, insep-

arable and practically limitless. Man is gaining
(or will gain) everything, without losing anything. Of course he can make mistakes, but these
very mistakes, sooner or later, will turn out to
his advantage. In other words, the communists
say that man is in process of continual self-
perfection—which means that today is inevitably
better than yesterday, tomorrow inevitably better than today. In all his activities man continues
to make progress, and it is this progress which
justifies his existence. We must also remember
that man has only just appeared on the surface
of the earth. What are three hundred thousand
years behind him compared to millions of years
still ahead? Man today is scarcely adolescent. He
is only now entering upon a period of full activity, I mean of complete awareness. And even
now he is still subject to the dream-life of his
childhood and it is well known that such dreams
are characterized by megalomania (for at certain
moments a child thinks he is capable of anything)
and by utter ineffectiveness. Man is only just beginning to be effective. How far will he advance,
or rather—for his progress is vertical—how high
will he lift himself? Already his attack on disease
is successful because he attacks it "scientifically";
will he not soon be attacking death itself, and no

less successfully since no less "scientifically"? At this rate, man will ultimately become some kind of angel.

It may not be useless to point out how reluctantly man—all men, of whatever faith—resigns himself to remaining what he is, to remaining motionless at any given point. Invariably, man aspires to something that he is not—at least, the man with a faith, the only difference between faiths being the different planes on which they promise their rewards. For either man presupposes a world above and beyond him to which he will be promoted, the world of pure spirit; or else, projecting into the future the material world in which he lives, he already sees himself as he will become after centuries have passed—by means of this law of progress which enables him, on his own impetus, to fulfill his destiny—so wholly freed of his present imperfections that he will enjoy a kind of angelic perfection. The angel is present everywhere. For either the angel, being timeless, is already in our world, or will enter our world tomorrow. Man is either spirit now or will become spirit. On the one hand, we see that the Christian or Mohammedan religions (to mention

only those two) classify the forms of life vertical-
ly like the rungs of a ladder, and proceed from
the mineral to the vegetable, from the vegetable
to the animal, from the animal to the human, and
then look up at the void which separates the
human from the divine, and fill that void with
celestial hierarchies. On the other hand, the
hypothesis of perpetual evolution starts with the
atom which then advances gradually, and without
any sudden break of continuity, until it finally
establishes at its peak such a domination over
matter that man, who is matter, can ultimately
enjoy, here on earth and in the flesh, beatitudes
which religion reserves for his resurrected body
after death. On the one hand, we have a stairway
with every human being living alone on his own
step, but with the possibility, through faith, of
a swift and final ascent; on the other hand, we
have a gently rising slope without beginning or
end up which all mankind advances by continual
progress until it is so changed as to be no longer
recognizable. Deep in their hearts, both the Christian and the materialist hold to hope, because it
is impossible for man not to hope; but, whereas
the Christian hopes for eternal life and thinks in
terms of personal consciousness, the materialist
considers personal consciousness completely in-

significant, an accidental result of something else, and not an enduring phenomenon. For the materialist, the human being does not count. There are no human beings, there are only individuals, and these are mere transients, here for a moment and then gone. So that it is in mankind as a whole that the materialist (rather oddly) places all his hope, or, more exactly, in an organized society of mankind; and he expects the realization of his hopes in a future which recedes indefinitely, since it is never defined.

How has it happened that a doctrine which teaches the nothingness of everything (this is certainly the materialist doctrine) makes a solitary exception in favor of mankind as an organized society? How is it that a doctrine so inherently pessimistic has reached an optimistic conclusion with regard to man's earthly destiny, by which I mean an optimistic view of life itself, and even a conception of existence in which enthusiasm (that is the only possible word)—for instance, enthusiasm for work—is not only preached, but is also practically obligatory? How has this doctrine, having destroyed man's faith in so many things through its pitiless labor of analysis, been able to restore faith to society; or, if not faith in the strict sense of the word, at least a kind of faith? For the postulates of materialism are infinitely tragic: we are born out of nothingness, and to nothingness we return. Not only do we ourselves, as conscious individuals, return to nothingness, but all we have built, thought and felt, all our inventions, everything alive, will also be plunged back, like ourselves, into unending night, and all will finally be as though it had never been.

It will be noticed that these ideas, in themselves no more than the logical conclusion to the philosophy of the French eighteenth century, are no different in their premises from the nihilism so fashionable fifty or sixty years ago. They were born in clouds of cigarette smoke on the banks of London's Thames, or Geneva's Arve, in the days of the earliest soviets—generally held in students' bedrooms and preferably between midnight and four in the morning. You can imagine those bearded gentlemen with their rumpled hair and eye-glasses; you can picture them, groups of ten or twelve sitting on camp beds, endlessly gesticulating—their hands too white (for they were not workmen, oh, not at all; they were the exact opposite of workmen in the best sense of that word, for they were pure "intellectuals"). They sat there arguing about God, as God was already argued about by Dostoevsky's characters whom they were imitating—and they concluded that God does not exist. Conclusion to the conclusion: nothing exists. Their young ladies were chaste; they wore high-collared shirtwaists. A samovar (an accidental remnant of nationalism which was otherwise barred from their doctrine) sang on the table. The young ladies took part in the debates. And the next day one of them would take cyanide. Nihil: nothing. Often they were beautiful; they were always in earnest. For the most part they lived in poverty; many had given all they possessed to the cause. What they retained was an extraordinary need for the absolute. So, one fine morning, they would drown themselves in the lake at Geneva or throw themselves into the Thames. "Nothing lasts and, knowing that nothing lasts, I cannot live"—was the practical conclusion they drew from the theory. Had they been of less noble nature they could have gone on living, enjoying the good things that fell to their lot and thus, day by day, like so many others, making the best of the advantages provided by a relativistic philosophy; but no, their souls were filled with "aspirations"—and it is true that eating and drinking do not suffice the soul.

It is this questioning of the soul which communism has suppressed. That is where the sleight-of-hand comes in. For communism denies that the soul has any needs at all, or rather, compelled to admit that they exist, it transposes them and claims to satisfy them by furnishing man with enough reasons to believe in himself and—aside from all metaphysics—to persevere in the effort, labor, and privation which constitute the grim life of those whom communism governs. The metaphysical concepts of communism are indeed very confused. Apparently man exists by chance, yet his existence is also strictly predetermined. And however strictly determined his existence, he nevertheless decides his own fate (he plans, he even makes five-year plans). Man is willed, but at the same time he wills. Man is merely a tiny gear in a gigantic mechanism, yet he has consciousness, since he claims to command the machinery. Thus, when you look more closely, you see that communism accumulates as the basis for its doctrine the most elementary metaphysical contradictions—which it entirely ignores or makes no effort to disentangle. Perhaps some day communism will clarify these contradictions, or perhaps they will resolve themselves.

Meanwhile the communist attitude is, or claims to be, strictly scientific—although it applies to the whole of life the disciplines which the scientist applies only to his work.

The only thing we know is the world. Let us take it as it is, and try to make the most of it, while mitigating as best we can the hardships imposed on us by nature. Communism has brought everything down in ruins, but its purpose is to rebuild. It has destroyed man's hope, yet it proclaims a hope (of another kind). We used to live on two different planes, but communism has kept only one. This is a fascinating aspect of communism: it is admittedly the first organized effort to make man live entirely on the plane of the material world, having completely undermined what till now has been man's chief hope. Perhaps communism loves life. We hope so. But it judges life only by appearances, by what life seems to be on the surface, and refuses to look for the roots— in a word, for the mystery. Communism does not believe in the mysterious; it claims that "the mysterious is only what we do not know now, but shall some day find out." Its hope lies in knowledge, in always knowing more.

Meanwhile, man must no longer ask himself where he comes from, what he is, or why he possesses some things and not others (actually he possesses nothing any more and is thus spared the need to ask). Man must no longer ask what his stature is, for there is no possible answer to the question; he must only ask what role he is to have in society. He must establish his place in society; his stature will be evaluated according to the role he plays.

Nothing exists except the State which is society, or society which is the State—since the two are one. The individual is only an organ of the State, or perhaps, more correctly, a gear of the State, since this form of state is apparently more mechanism than organism. The State's interest in the individual is confined to his usefulness, his daily output. The State does the thinking for the individual and the State's activity is the sum of the activities it exacts from each individual, according to an overall plan—for example, the famous five-year plan. The individual only exists as a part of the social whole and, in the last analysis, the social whole takes the place of the human being and measures itself against the universe.

But man measures himself, is in fact obliged to measure himself against the task imposed upon him which he must accept. Nothing is so suspect to the constituted authorities and the responsible leaders of the Soviet régime as what they call "solitary ruminations"—in other words, the attempts man makes to measure himself against the world and face a reality beyond him.

Collectively, mankind is enveloped in a kind of caul inside which it is one day destined to reach final fulfillment; and for the régime there is no more serious crime than an effort to break through this caul to see what lies outside—since this presupposes the possibility of something outside it. Needless to say, communist ideology starts by taking great pains to assure you that there is nothing else. Communism alone can know, decide, and teach. A person who knows and decides for himself, or even claims the right to do so, automatically becomes a rival of communism— an intolerable rival, and one, moreover, they do not tolerate. Communism delegates its powers to special groups created to deal with technical and scientific matters, but makes it abundantly clear that all research undertaken by these groups must be subordinated from the start to an ideology, the communist ideology, and is only valid when it confirms that ideology. "Stop thinking," communism tells the individual, "you are incapable of independent thought."

In our time, thinking is done by instruments

116

and mathematical formulae. Communism opposes nothing so strongly as contemplation, or anything remotely akin to contemplation. For what is contemplation, if not *personal* contact with a reality which is entirely subjective and therefore evades all social controls? The most interesting thing to observe is the way communist society, sharply aware of the dangers inherent in any form of contemplation, tries to forestall it by ridiculing the contemplative nature—since, according to the communists, the contemplative is an ill man, and therefore useless. Hence even the recognized poet must become a man of action and must serve the cause; while potential poets, dreamers—so many of whom must still be hidden in that vast land which seems so right for them—are considered victims of neurasthenia, fit only for medical care. When a man feels the need of questioning himself, it is proof of neurasthenia; indeed, the fact that he feels the need to be alone is proof of illness. The Soviets see to it that no one is ever alone, and in this they are obviously successful since the inhabitants of their cities are alloted only ten square meters apiece, and a five-room apartment often houses as many as five families. Communism loves itself exclusively; it therefore demands from everyone this same

117

exclusive love. It offers man the worship of an ideology; in fact, it allows him to worship nothing else.

★

The season of restless nights has come again, when once again the winds of spring are blowing. I can understand being an atheist; I cannot understand being content to be an atheist. The winds of spring blow year after year, yet a time will come when they will blow no longer, nor any longer will there be a spring, nor any season; the winds are persistent and lasting, yet they are destined to final stillness. A time will come, therefore, when these strong spring winds no longer carry the fine tang of sap and also of snow—a tang which somehow fuses what is soon to come with what is already passing. There will be a time when nothing more can come into being, when all that now exists shall no longer be. In the middle of the night, lying on my back, I keep very still. There is one more strong gust of wind, and then the wind falls with a thud like a bird with a broken wing. After that there is nothing to be heard, only a hush everywhere, and I, too, am silent. Everything is motionless, and I, too, am still. It is as though there were nothing left alive here within my four walls, and I do not move. I am doing nothing, I am concerned only with existing, and all the more preoccupied with it because, for the moment, I am doing nothing else. I am not trying to change anything, and nothing, apparently, is in process of change around me. I am merely existing, completely inactive, completely alone.

This must be the hour when, outside the carefully closed windows and the closely drawn curtains of my room, a little quarter moon takes advantage of the stillness to appear between two clouds and whiten the parts of the earth on which it looks down. It is the time of the white frosts, a time when the moon makes the most of its powdery light to change the color of the grass, still yellow at this season but turning green, and of the earth, still gray but turning dark, and of the upper sides of the very small leaves beginning to open here and there on the rambler rose-bushes. This whole process takes place in silence. Possibly something is happening outside my windows, but nothing is happening where I am, here in the heavy darkness where nothing exists but myself. Even the mouse has ceased rattling nuts in its hiding-place between the beams of the ceiling. Nothing is happening here in the silence where there is neither a woman, nor memory of women, nor even that obstinate pursuit of a phrase which, of all loves, is surely the least rewarding, the most obsessive. All I now feel is the bare fact that I am alive.

When the wind falls so abruptly in the night, when buds are bursting in silence, when birds are beginning to sing, timidly and still uncertainly (their song is soon silenced again by the night), when everything in nature is hastening toward life—at this hour you are happy to realize that you do not even know what life is. At this hour you listen only to the sound of a voice speaking within you, telling you that you are alive, and you believe that voice.

In the deep of the night, lying on my back, I ask myself what life is and I see that I do not know; but I also see that it is a royal thing to be alive. Royal: I write the word and I do not know what it means. I do not even write the word; my pen forms the letters, but the word comes of itself.

Out of the boundless immensity of what could or might exist we can grasp but a few realities. We see only what exists, only a few things that have actual existence: stars, planets, gases, solids and liquids, and the organic life of which we are one form. But why are we a part of life? That is what we do not understand. For if anything at all exists, why does not everything exist? Why is the world an ever-changing series of states of being—at least the world we know? Yet there is this point in time, this place where I now am, this instant which is only temporary, but in which I now exist and, as I lie here holding on to this fact, I take a lasting pleasure in it.

I am a transient in time and space, yet I am suddenly unable to think of myself as temporary, for existence is so precious a thing that it seems impossible for it to end. Suddenly existence seems endless: the instant contains eternity.

Royal: that is the prerogative of a king. A king survives—but then everything survives, everything is lasting, everything persists, everything desires to survive, nothing consents to end.

You will tell me: "All this is pure childishness." Of course it is. You will add: "It is futile." And I agree; it leads nowhere. All sensible people, all reasonable people, will doubtless maintain that nothing is so futile as to raise questions which you know will not be answered. These sensible people are right. They have every right to object to the futility of a mind either unoccupied or busy threshing chaff, unaware that the grain is gone. It is true that I am accomplishing nothing, busy with nothing; I am lying here stretched out on my back. At this hour everything is asleep, both men and things, while as for me, I lie idly dreaming about this humanity and this material world which might well not have been, yet are. Agonized yet delighted, fearful yet also astounded, how can I not turn toward them once again and ask, out of the depths of the unknowable, the meaning of life? There was a time when they did not exist, and now they are here; they exist now, but there will come a time when they will no longer be here. Who calls them into the light of existence? And why, having enjoyed the light of existence, are they destined to return into the night of nothingness? Yet still the fact remains that I myself am alive, if only for a brief while longer. I recognize my own existence and I measure what I am; I have a beginning and an end; I have height, width, weight. I touch this body, I know that it has weight, that it fills space, that it is instinct with motion and warmth, and that it has a conscious longing to know all things, even the unknowable—especially the unknow-

122

able. And this in itself is a kind of greatness. Am I master of these thoughts of mine which fly out in all directions and, like bees escaping from the hive, go, not where I tell them to, but where they please? Moreover, they go where they know there is no use in going, they bring back no pollen, they return no richer than before. Yet it is royal (I use the word again) to seek the very substance of life and not the accidental, to go straight to the principle of life and not to its attributes, to pursue all that cannot be known of life rather than the little that can, to reach what must be called its mystery—and rejoice in this mystery rather than feel humiliated by it. For one can love the mystery that is life and those who love it show a form of greatness. Or one can hate it, seeing in it only a limitation imposed upon man. And, possibly, in that attitude also there is a kind of greatness, but another kind of greatness. No doubt these two kinds of greatness are irreconcilable, for the one proceeds from acceptance while the other is based on refusal, and while hate leads to revolt and can serve a purpose, or claims that some day it will serve a purpose, love cannot be put to any use at all.

In the deep of the night we let loose the swarm of our thoughts, without the slightest concern for utility. They go off into the void, quite uselessly questioning the void, for this questioning is futile. Could it be, perhaps, that what we call the void is, after all, simply the total of what exists, and that this fullness of existence is itself the void? We let our thoughts wander, not expecting them to return with answers. In the unknown and unknowable we can see only that one thing has been given us: life itself. It does not matter much what life has brought us, or what life holds in reserve for us; it does not matter what kind of life we have, or whether it has been, as they say, kind or cruel. We are alive; that is the extraordinary thing. Alone in the silent night, resting when all sounds are hushed, when the trivial and the incidental have become remote, it is then that we are supremely conscious that we live, and grateful to be alive.

Some men are grateful to be alive and others are not.

Does gratitude presuppose an absolute?

Some curse life while they endure it; some are indifferent toward life, I mean toward the fact that they are alive. Some bless life, no matter what it brings them. Whom do they bless? They do not know.

Something, or someone?

They do not know. But they know that at the source of their being there is a greatness to which they are linked. And they are unwilling to abandon the hope that they will share finally in that greatness again.

MAN AND NATURE

WHAT WE must first try to gauge is the extent to which nature (or what we call nature) is outside ourselves. If we say that nature is everything in the universe that has nothing to do with man, everything that is independent of man, everything that does not know man and is often unknown to him, we cannot avoid seeing that its autonomy has now been seriously encroached upon. It then becomes important to consider to what further extent this autonomy will be encroached upon in the future, for man, after all, has only just begun to imperil it. What, if any, are the limits to man's powers? Beyond doubt they are steadily increasing while there is a corresponding decline in the autonomy of nature's forces. That is the great question. It bears fundamentally on our political opinions, and the way we answer it lies at the root of contemporary man's attitude toward life itself. Man can accomplish everything—or nothing. Either he believes that all things are subject to his will, if not now, then surely later; or, on the contrary, he believes that there is little he can do because of the forces of nature and, ultimately, because of God. Some men—the men of the Left—think that we shall end by mastering nature, but others think that too much meddling with nature will provoke a reaction, sudden and violent, which will bring about our end. Faith in man, faith in something which surpasses man: these are the two real poles, the Left, the Right (since the use of these terms today seems unavoidable). This makes it easy to explain the well-known phenomenon by which all political parties move gradually from Right to Left as a direct result of the ever-increasing confidence man places in his own powers (greatly encouraged by science) and thus it is merely the political and sociological aspect of a far more general shift in belief from the omnipotence of nature (that was the past) to the omnipotence of man (which is the present, or the future). Do I believe in this future, this limitless future, or not? Do I believe in progress, in continual progress, or not?

What human faculty can answer these questions? Man's reason? Reason is incapable of providing an answer. No answer is valid unless one first believes that it is valid. In other words, faith alone can provide the answer. And if it is only through faith that we find an answer, then today there is not less, but far more faith on the Left than on the Right. The Left believes in a cause; the Right used to believe in a Person, but now believes no longer, or at least inadequately. This inadequacy is all the greater because the Right exploited its beliefs with considerable imprudence and attributed to God or nature—thereby endowing them with a sacred character—many phenomena which may not come from God and may not exist in nature: such phenomena as nations, the institutions of the family and property and, no doubt, money and war—and for many on the Right, even banks, I imagine, and certainly the army and, needless to say, religion. Thus they set up a wall behind which, without even believing in its fabric, they have taken cover, and now stubbornly defend their special privileges and what they call the established order which of course is only one form of order, but an order with the advantage—for them—of maintaining unchanged a system by which they profit.

What is in nature and what is not in nature? The men of the Left say: "Nothing is in nature but what we allow to remain there." For it is clear that nature's autonomy is steadily shrinking, at least on the earth's surface. Nature still keeps its entire autonomy in space where man does not interfere except to observe the course of the stars through his telescope, except to acquire knowledge. Although space is more or less known to him, he cannot yet exploit it. Man does not harness the stars nor has he yet managed to set them to work for him, and the stars are part of nature, of course.

But a waterfall is also part of nature. How many waterfalls in our European countries still fall freely? Everywhere on our mountainsides they have been tracked down and captured, imprisoned behind dams, walled up in steel pipes. They have all been put to use, or will be soon, but no longer in a simple and direct way for, and here is the essential point, they are no longer used as the peasant used them when he set a wheel beneath them with a mill beside it. Instead they are used indirectly; their power is transformed into electricity carried along wires and made to turn every conceivable kind of engine, furnishing motion, heat and light—which are all one and the same thing. In the beginning man made use of nature, yet he used it empirically, remained subject to it, dependent on it; in other words, if the water stopped falling on the wheel, the wheel stopped turning.

Thus man's powers were limited, and it is only recently, through science and analysis, that he has learned to follow link by link the long chain of causality, and thus penetrate the innermost life of phenomena. Or if I may put it this way, man is no longer simply in contact with one extremity of the chain of natural forces, as when he used them without modifying them in any way; he is now engaged in tracing these forces back to a central point where he finds they all converge and discovers that their energy has a single source; that their secret, which he is about to penetrate, lies in their common origin. Knowing the nature of that origin, nothing can stop him from finally bending all these forces to his will. Man used the waterfall just as he found it, to turn the wheel of his mill; then he harnessed it and transformed its energy; and now, discovering that energy is everywhere, he no longer busies himself with the waterfall but with the constituent parts of the waterfall, and he finds that they are motionless; he discovers that where there is the greatest immobility—by a sort of prodigious paradox—there is also the greatest energy. And now it is the atom that he hungrily approaches, the atom which is held in a vise by its own terrible force. Here is modern man.

But the true peasant is pre-eminently the man who uses nature's forces directly. He made an early appearance on the earth and he is still here, little changed, but more and more shaken, more and more battered by economic necessities and by all the machines these necessities require. He was, and still is, a complete human being who by his own effort drew nourishment from the land on which he lived and was therefore able to be independent. The peasant was able to live, that is to say he nourished himself, sheltered himself, clothed himself, from his own resources; he was able to satisfy his essential needs—for man has needs that are essential and others that are not. He has needs which must be met—the need to eat and drink—or else he dies. And after these he has other needs, many of them, which he himself gradually creates to embellish or broaden his life (and here he is quite capable of making mistakes). But these needs are artificial; they do not profoundly affect his existence and he can suppress them, and indeed is often obliged to suppress them. The peasant is the man who best provided for essential human needs, and who drew directly from nature to satisfy his own needs. For when there are machines you have industry, and the peasant who uses machinery becomes a mechanic.

The peasant took his techniques from nature: for power he used his own strength, or the strength of the horse and the ox, or the llama, the elephant, the camel. He invented the wheel, which eludes the weight placed on it by continually turning so that it only weighs on the ground at one changing point. He invented a tool, that is merely a prolongation of man's arms and legs, which is merely the hardening of man's nails: a tool such as the hoe, which provides one long metal blade to replace his ten thinly protected fingers. He invented the idea of using a longer or shorter haft for his axe to increase the force of the blow. The saw, the hammer, the pitchfork— all these inventions simply reproduce, and perfect, the natural means at his disposal. Armed with these tools, surrounded by his flocks (having taken into his life the animals which could haul for him or give him their wool or their milk and "domesticated" them), surrounded also by his family working beside him—he really created a natural group, independent of men, but on the other hand depending entirely on the earth and sky. Peasant life was patriarchal; the further we move away from patriarchal life, the further we move away from the peasant. Helped and sustained by his family, the peasant had to deal with almost nothing else but nature. Now, however, he is obliged to deal with an increasingly mechanized existence which separates him both from nature and his family, or at least changes to a great extent the relationship he once had with both. He lived on the soil, and sought only to improve it, to render it more productive. He looked up to the sky and suffered the cold, the heat, the dark, and the unvarying course of the seasons; he accepted the climate, without seeking to change it as man so elaborately seeks to do today, for he thought of it as an unalterable fact which he had to face—and perhaps also propitiate.

Once again I see you standing there in the open and, no matter what they say about you, peasant, you have been great. You are bowed down over the earth; the sky is bright above you; later the light fades. Bending, straightening up, bending again, for how many centuries have you obstinately been working the soil, this soil baked hard by the sun, drowned and washed away by the rain? You walk on it and it is so hard that you can hear yourself walking on it, or else it sticks to your feet, adding a heavy weight to the soles of your boots; and you are bound to it, completely bound to it, wholly dependent on it, entirely enslaved by it, and all you can do with it is determined for you by sun, or lack of sun; but behind the sun there used to be the gods, there used to be God. And today? That resignation of yours could have existed fully only because you also had faith in reality, and you worshipped it; when faith no longer exists, there can no longer be resignation, for resignation is love. You patiently endured the changing seasons, since you did not cause them and could not control them, and they succeeded each other through endless winter, spring, burning summer, autumn; turning round the axis of the year like the four little cars on the carrousel at the fair, painted gray, green, yellow, red, always appearing and disappearing in the same order, with their promise, their threat, their caprices—though sometimes they keep their promise, for after all there are years when the wine is good and the crops are good—but you never can be sure in advance.

But you, peasant, like a child playing hide-and-seek, you had your turn at waiting in your corner to be found. Having taken all possible precautions, there was nothing you could do but wait. Having done your share, all your share, you waited. Having labored, you crossed your hands on the haft of your hoe and rested, leaning upon it, while you searched the sky where your fate would be decided by no rain or too much rain, by clear weather or hail. You had staked your whole existence on a hope that was often disappointed —though not always; you had put your trust in something over which you had no control, in something that you could not know but which you accepted.

Centuries passed.

Great civilizations came and they were founded on your understanding of the world, an understanding based on perseverance, patience and resignation, but also on trust.

It is common knowledge that you were avaricious, a sharp bargainer, often hard on others, but also hard on yourself. You rose early and it was late when you slept; when you were planting or harvesting it was not six hours you worked, or even eight, but twelve and fourteen and sixteen hours on end. And for everything you depended on the sky and the stars, watching the most beloved of them all—the most useful, the one best known to you—rise above the horizon in the east, fall beneath the horizon in the west, following its course from year's start to year's end. You cried out: "The sun is rising!" and you said: "And now it has set." But there was this intimacy between you, though the sun was often your enemy: when it shone too steadily, drying out the grass to the roots, or when it shone only intermittently and no longer stirred life in the grass and the grass did not grow. But you felt a basic harmony everywhere, since to be a peasant is not a profession but a condition, something that lasts, something that seems always to have existed, something that one does not expect to abandon, that one does not even think it possible to abandon, something handed down from father to child. For it never occurred to you that the sun could change, or ever had changed. You were bound to a natural way of living that, you thought, nothing could alter; and afterwards—but only afterwards —there could be men who lived in other ways; poets, painters, sculptors, musicians, architects. You had built a certain kind of house to suit your needs, and you were incapable of imagining that there could be other kinds of houses—by which I mean, other needs. You had a certain slowness, a certain prudent way of meting out your effort in order to give to each of your motions the rhythm which made it possible for you to keep on repeating it as long as there was need. You did not talk much; you rested at times in the shade of a tree. Your life was a blend of action and contemplation, in which contemplation was also action, since you kept on thinking about your work even when you were not working; and in which action was also contemplation, since while you moved, while your body toiled, your mind remained free, and in the open air, in the wind, your mind contemplated the sky and sea. For you there was no real break between work and rest. The two were so merged that, for instance, you did not change your clothes when you had finished your work, you did not change into city clothes by putting on a coat and tie, like the workman leaving the factory. All you did was to wash your hands, and then you came out to sit on the bench in front of your house with your children round you. You did not play at any games, you had no need of entertainment; you watched while everything about you was at play: the leaves on the tree, the animals, everything that lived; your children playing at hide-and-seek, the kitten playing with the ball of wool, the birds playing before they went to sleep.

140

There were six days and then came Sunday because, for you, there was God and the day that belonged to God—God whom perhaps you did not know, but whom you at least accepted, and so it was all right for the church bells to ring out across the fields while you dressed yourself up. On Sundays you dressed yourself up and you shaved, out of respect for God; you put on a white shirt, a black tie, usually clothes that were black or dark gray, your Sunday hat—all this because of a certain veneration you felt and tried to show by the clothes you put on, peasant of our climates, peasant of our villages; and the women also put on their best dresses, their silk aprons, and tied colored kerchiefs round their necks.

For veneration was still abroad in the world: even in Hesiod's day the traveler was told to salute the calm flowing river before crossing it. The peasant venerated a person or a thing: behind the lightning was Jupiter, behind the waves, Neptune. The peasant lived in a world everywhere inhabited not only by himself or by men like himself, but by certain presences or by a single great Presence.

It was these presences, or this one Presence, that the poets sang, the painters painted, the sculptors carved; picturing man, and at the same

141

time the presences surrounding him, fearful and threatening, yet raising his stature by forcing him to surpass himself; both frightening and reassuring him, for they were all-powerful indeed, but they heard man's prayer. There were the gods, or there was God, and they were on your side once you had obeyed their commands, once they had been appeased by sacrifice or prayer. The heifer bled on the altar; above the altar two hands raised the Host. At fixed and recurrent seasons, a general absolution descended upon man and suddenly he found himself in harmony with an eternal and excellent order to which he belonged.

This participation was collective, for it brought men together who lived far apart and it gathered them round a certainty common to them all. They were not mustered to work every morning by a factory siren nor at nightfall disbanded when the siren blew again. Once a week they were called by the steeple bells which came from far across the fields to mingle with the hum of insects, the chatter of birds in the trees. That is still the way it is, all over our countrysides of the West. From every point on the horizon at the hour of Mass the peasants whose dwellings are so far apart hasten over their mountain paths, or along the roads of the plain, forming all those little points in the landscape, at first scattered, and then, as they approach, coming closer together and finally converging. They are all united as they kneel together, because of a faith which they all share. And it has been that way from the time of the Egyptians to our own day. They are separated and then united; separated all through the week, united on Sunday; and then they return to their separate homes, which are surrounded by the fields they work—and the fields separate them from other homes. They follow an ancient way of life and the civilization based on this way of life is ancient too, and both depend wholly on nature. It is the life you see painted in the tombs of the Pharaohs where all those little red men with sickles stand before a field of wheat resembling a wall; the life you read about in Genesis; the life you find again in the Duc de Berry's *Book of Hours* where the women spin their wool while tending their flocks; it is a life which still persists today in many parts of the world. But how long will it last?

For the true peasant is vanishing. And if he has not already vanished, if he still survives, it is due —in Europe, at least—to the protective measures adopted by the nations at their frontiers. The peasant only survives as a small landowner and

producer, because our countries, anxious to keep
their internal equilibrium, have adopted—and
indeed have been forced to adopt—a system of
artificial checks and balances, such as putting an
almost prohibitive duty on butter, milk, livestock,
fodder, paying premiums to wheat growers, fixing
minimum prices. Only by this system has the
peasant been kept going (and barely); although
the system is doubtless costly to the consumer, it
helps to keep a balance which, however arbitrary, looks solid in the light of the dire upheav-
als we fear. The peasant therefore owes his survival to these laws and regulations. Little by little
—he is still unaware of it, but for how much
longer—he has become a museum piece, something outlived, a sort of keepsake, worth preserv-
ing as best we can—but how much longer can we
preserve it? Such relics are expensive and the
time will doubtless come when nations cannot
afford them. For we are already at the point
where we need only lower the tariff a little, reduce the premiums paid to producers, cut the
minimum prices paid to farmers—to ruin the
entire peasant economy.

Everywhere science and industry work against
the peasant: science, which substitutes analysis
for empiricism, and industry, which uses the

methods of science, together producing the same results. We have the Canadian wheat factories, the Brazilian coffee factories, the Soviet kolkhoz; we have the régime of the tractor and the dividing up of the world into zones of specialized production. It was to the peasant's advantage to produce all he needed in one place; it is to the advantage of industry, which has such vast expenses and such an enormous potential as a result of the perfecting of machinery, to spread out its production: here wheat and there wine, here dairy products and there vegetables. Thus industrial production and peasant production are at cross-purposes, and so, too, are the true peasant and the peasant-mechanic who is gradually replacing him. The true peasant has always stayed put. He has never heard the term "operating unit"—though he and his family form one. He holds only as much land as he can cultivate alone or with the help of his wife and children or with one or two hired hands who count as part of the family. But the peasant-mechanic is only a day-laborer, no longer dependent on the land. One month he may be harvesting, but the next he may be in a factory making machine guns. He is no longer in direct contact with matter, with nature itself; his hands set gears in motion, but it is the gears which act directly. Moreover, there are no two things so opposite as the machine and the tool. The tool is only useful when the man who holds it works hard and well, for it derives its force from the man; whereas a well-constructed machine runs by itself, is a force outside man, and only needs man to supervise its mechanism—always the same mechanism, whether it turns shells or reaps and binds wheat. We are just beginning this industrial exploitation of nature but its goal is already apparent: the mastery of nature by methods drawn from nature itself.

For instance, since weather cannot always be relied on, industry has substituted for sunlight a heating system of its own, underground or overhead, and can thus grow magnificent cucumbers in the middle of winter. Whether the soil is rich or poor, industry can now obtain from chemistry a perfect synthetic equivalent. Though night follows day, industry can produce an artificial light which ingeniously fuses the life-giving rays to ripen a cluster of grapes in a week. The grape is no longer permitted to rest twelve hours out of every twenty-four; the grape is *forced* to ripen. The cucumber does not wait till July appears on the calendar; the cucumber is told that it is July all year round and believes, or seems to believe,

146

what it is told. The cucumber too is *forced* to ripen—and does not appear to realize that it is being forced. In all innocence plants and vegetables have submitted to the new laws made by man, laws of his own which he has substituted for the laws of nature, and this very submission seems to prove that man has at least understood the basis of nature's laws. But how far will nature let itself be penetrated? Will the day not come when nature takes its revenge? Or is nature's apparent submissiveness—as the men of the Left keep saying—nothing but a sign of relief at receiving man's help and protection, and of willingness to produce more and more abundantly with more and more haste? The central drama of our times is that man is now moving away from his primary powers toward his secondary powers, from his direct powers to his indirect powers. He is using these new powers to the utmost and no one can foretell where the exploitation of these tremendous powers will lead him: whether to total ruin, or toward a total renewal of himself, towards a new self-confidence, a new upsurge of pride, and new material advantages which will finally enable him to fulfill his dream of complete mastery over matter by fathoming, through the analysis of cause and effect, the last, secret depths of the *how* of this world.

Starting at every point along the world's circumference, man has steadily moved toward its mechanical center (but perhaps everything is mechanical). What we see today, therefore, is a fascinating spectacle of centripetence: the various sciences, having been developed independently, now converging to form one major science, with chemistry, physics and the mechanical sciences merged together. It is like watching the completing of a picture-puzzle in which the first pieces took millions of years to be fitted into place, while the last pieces, each of which shows clearly where it is cut to join the others, can be fitted together instantaneously--to the great astonishment of the onlooker.

But in this effort to mechanize the world the spectators of the game are also involved. Whether they want to or not, they are playing the game themselves. Their possessions, their bodies, their souls are at stake; indeed their very lives. Therefore they have to take sides. They do not yet see what will happen when the puzzle has been completed; either they accept it sight unseen and are delighted because they believe in it—the Leftist point of view—or they suspect and fear it because they believe in something else, and that is the point of view of the Right.

Exactly what will happen to the peasant and the land when agriculture has been industrialized?

Judging by certain recent phenomena, we can perhaps surmise what will happen to the land, for a soil is rich or poor, grows some things and not others, is flat or uneven.

The whole world will be plotted out in enormous production zones: there will be the wheat zone and the rice zone, the zones for vegetables, for fruit trees and vineyards, and in each of these zones real factories will be set up for the production of wheat, rice, vegetables, fruit and wine. They say the time will come when whole cities move to the country and it might well happen, but only because by that time the country will have become a city, at least the productive part of the country, where the topography, the quality of the soil, and the transportation facilities prove specially valuable.

The rest will be abandoned. Already the France of small farms is disappearing. One remembers the sight of all those abandoned villages in the Cévennes. You can still see on the hillsides the little walls which used to support those tiers of square vine-plots, those little fields of wheat and rye that are now crumbling away among the thickets. You can see houses split in two from top to bottom, with one half fallen down. You look into a room on the second floor, open like a doll's house, and you see the remains of a bed. You say: "Why did he leave his furniture behind?" "He" means the former proprietor. "Well," someone answers, "he got a job on the railroad a long way from here . . . he figured that it would cost more to take the furniture than it was worth. And here there was no one to buy it."

The city has already invaded the country and it is safe to say that it will invade it still more, with its machinery and its customs. The repair shops along the roads belong to the city, and the filling stations belong to the city, and so too does the speed of the automobiles driving along the roads. There will be immense urban regions (in the country) and between these regions there will be spaces that are still virgin or have returned to a kind of virginity, that is to their natural state. These will be uninhabited national reservations into which we shall see the city people stream every weekend and perhaps fall back from their state of ultra-civilization to a bare state of nature.

Man needs nature. Either one half of him is constantly in contact with nature, dividing him from himself but also giving him a certain equilibrium, or else he is completely deprived of nature for long periods and then must make up for this deprivation by plunging back into it for a time. That is why men go on camping trips and become nudists.

When the country has been made into a city, people will leave their apartments on the twentieth floor with all the modern improvements of gas, electricity, hot and cold running water, warmed or cooled air, garbage chutes, radios, and electric ice-boxes, and camp out stark naked in a man-made desert.

★

There are men who seek in nature an escape. Some of the best of these seek God in nature. They turn to nature only because they believe that nature proves the existence of God. Such men seem somewhat more prevalent in little countries like ours than elsewhere, chiefly because nature is beautiful here, or considered beautiful, or at any rate these men think it beautiful. But they are apt to neglect our forests, meadows and vineyards, the shores of our lakes; theirs is an exclusive love—for the high mountains. What they are fleeing is man, because man prevents them from finding what they seek, which is God. They know that the higher they climb, the further they are from man; they scale the heights where man no longer lives and leave mankind far below.

Remember, friends of my youth, those Saturday mornings. In those days I was one of you. Remember how carefully we prepared our trips: the knapsack, the studded boots, the ice-axe, the coiled rope (the best ropes, I think, were the red ones), before we started out. Now I stay at home, but when Saturday comes you still set forth at dawn. You have become professors or lawyers or doctors, and I have become nothing. Although the years, many years, have gone by, the high mountains still call you and you are still faithful to the jackets made out of raw Valais wool, to those supposedly waterproof Tyrolese cloths, to a certain type of crampon for your boots, to a particular make of ice-axe.

You still pursue nature, one special kind of nature; I rather think that what you still hope to find is the same thing you have always sought.

I admit all the benefits of physical exercise. I admit that in some of you there is a concern for hygiene which is wholly respectable—your need of "fresh air" and your need of "action." I know that most of you have sedentary habits, that you sit almost all the time, and that to sit so much makes one long to stand. I also know that there is the technical side, the satisfaction of overcoming difficulty, and that mountain climbing, with its schools, its systems and its theories, is a career in itself. And I am well aware that these trips provide escape from the boredom of daily life, a life which only appears at its best when you can occasionally break away from the worries at home or at the office, from harassing preoccupations, and be free, and that, although the problems are still there when you return, they weigh less heavily for having been dropped, if only for a time. The high mountains, for many of those who frequent them, serve as pretext to escape. But are they only an escape? Are there not also contemplative people for whom action in itself is of little or no importance; for whom action is only a means, a physical means to "raise" themselves—the word "raise" having two meanings which here coincide.

I am thinking of those religious minds for whom material height is no more than the symbol for another kind of height. They climb far, they

toil upward until they reach the summit of a
peak, and there they sit down, two or three men
together, or one man alone, smoking pipes. And
here they dominate. What do they dominate? The
physical world—but not just the physical world;
they dominate all matter. Confounding the idea
of material greatness with omnipotence, the idea
of beauty with goodness, they contemplate the
world from far above it. From far above they contemplate the works of God—no longer held apart
from Him by anything, since He is there with
them, high above His creation. They are like the
astronomer who studies the motion of the stars
through the silent night. He discovers at the end
of his telescope the mathematical order of the
universe—and considers himself symbolically a
part of it.

But what they see is certainly not order; it is
the most extreme disorder. It is an organic disorder, and so, from their heights, they organize it
into beauty. What is beauty? They think they
have found the source of beauty; they are "edi-
fied" by the mountain tops. Collapse and ruin lie
round and about and below them, but in a harmonious whole. The bare rock sparkles and rises
in the air, all bathed in light. The rock is rose-
colored, it is like silver, it is like ivory. It is naked,

154

resplendent in its nakedness. It is like a woman's body warmly tinted by the sun, indolently stretched out on the velvet of the fields, recumbent, drowsing or half raised, leaning on one elbow and resting upon this blue, impalpable, multi-colored couch of light and shadow, while the men on the mountain-top look down at these endless circles of light and shadow, and there is this remoteness and this peace. Here they are, and on three sides the abyss yawns beneath them. To the left a mist billows up and it is the color of ripe fruit; but before them and to the right, the depths are cold and dark and empty. What is this feeling of calm which emanates from the abyss?

What organized the disorder? The men on the mountain top say it is God. How is it that what is forever crumbling and perishing, forever returning to nothingness, should suggest to them the idea of eternity and the creator of the eternal— as well as the creator of the fleeting? For it is indeed the creator of the perishable whom these men contemplate and worship; what they worship, looking down at this chaos, is a creator.

Behind them lies the steep and narrow ridge by which they reached the summit, and the snow where they stepped is marked a deeper translucent blue. They are suspended above everything.

Beneath them on three sides hangs the void. To east, and west, and north, they survey a succession of peaks and crags and glaciers; here the mountain is hollowed into a valley, flat or rolling, and there it suddenly climbs again, sheer but cleft in all directions, with a sharp rise and then a chasm. Over it all reigns majestic silence.

The men are there, hooded in this silence, yet the silence is never complete. Somewhere stones have broken loose and the moving air carries the sound of their distant fall and it is gentle, like the sound you hear when a man is raking gravel on a path; or the sound of a torrent is heard for a moment and then no more; or the wind itself is heard like the sound of a sail filling suddenly, the canvas snapping taut; or there is a sound like a muffled cough, a rumble, a growl, hardly perceptible yet threatening, like an uneasy watchdog stirring in the night. Then again they hear nothing, nothing and yet all these sounds. But what they think they hear, these men on the mountain top, is neither the sounds nor the silence; what they think they hear is a hymn of joy and gratitude rising from the created to the creator.

What is nature's relation to man? What is nature's relation to God?

Either God is in nature, and does not know

us; or else He knows us, and is not in nature.

If God is love, what does He love? If He is total good, how can He make Himself one with nature, which contains both good and evil?

Here, once again, I allude of course to our well-known trait, which began by identifying the love of one's native land with nationalism, and now no longer distinguishes between love of nature and love of God. No more is God simply praised in His works; His existence is now proved by His works. At this point it would be useful for the Christian to reread Pascal: "I am amazed at the boldness with which certain people undertake to speak of God. Addressing their tract to the unbeliever, their first chapter will prove the existence of a Divinity through the works of nature.... The God of nature could not possibly be the God of Grace. . . . Those who (relying only on man's intelligence) seek out everything in nature which might lead them to a knowledge of God, find only obscurity and darkness. . . . The God of Grace is a hidden God."

The God of Grace must be a hidden God, and not a God whom all can look upon, for a God whom all could see would tend to annul the hidden God and, by His immanence in nature, would oppose the transcendent God, the God Whose existence these friends of nature think that, through nature, they are discovering. For what does nature say? Nature says that it is sufficient unto itself. Nature proclaims its own eternity—a different eternity, an eternity within time, for the atom within time is eternal. All that nature builds is transitory; but the materials with which nature builds do not vanish, for they are gaseous, or not even gaseous—since they originate in the sources of gases and return eventually to their origins (at least that is what science affirms). Nature cannot exist except within the limits of time and space; but the God of Christians exists outside time and space.

There are men who refuse to see that nature does absolutely everything that their religion forbids them to do; nature kills, and their religion forbids them to kill; nature means continual warfare, and their religion stands against wars of any kind.

There are men who go to the mountains to admire them. They do not know mountains well. For although all nature is violent, in the mountains it reaches a peak of violence, a climax of instability, since here the heights are drawn to the depths in an unending process of ruin which destroys not only the mountains themselves but all they encounter: the mountain destroys while being itself destroyed. Here in the mountains there is hardly anything that does not die by violence; though men will go to any lengths (with all sorts of laws) to combat murder and make sure that we die only the death we call—not without irony —a natural death. For man, unable to assure his survival after death, tries at least to postpone as long as possible its coming. Here, in the mountains, everything yields to the law of the survival of the strongest. The cliff crumbles into the high pastures, the high pastures slide down into the torrent. The torrent is held back for a long time by the dam but, as soon as it can, it breaks through and drags with it the whole valley. The valley falls into the plain; the plain, in turn, is eroded and gradually carried off into the sea.

We console ourselves too easily; too easily we praise these mountains which are but the symbol of our fate. For all they tell us is that we too shall end. Man has science on his side, but the mountain has force; man's science can ensnare force and use it, but cannot master it. So when I climb the mountain and look down, I see only the eagle circling on motionless wing, the eagle of the high Alps, the ravisher of lambs (Lämmergeier), the eagle which, they told us as children, comes down even to our villages to snatch babies from their cradles; and below the eagle there is only the arm of a glacier hanging from a cleft rock, sombre, streaked with azure rifts, suspended there, proud and savage. The eagle follows its own law; the glacier follows it own law. Above these laws there is the law of laws—that we must constantly move on from more life to less life; that we must watch everything fall, ourselves included; that we are unceasingly drawn downward as the mountain is drawn downward, a process we can see as the waters pour down the mountain and drag it with them. And now, listen: what is this ceaseless laughter, this unending mockery, this whispering, this rumbling—when a little stone yields to its weight and rolls down the hill; when the avalanche starts to slide, leaving a higher point for a lower; when the glacier itself cracks in half, or when a block of ice formed by the glacier hangs trembling and sways like a tree and then falls with its roots upturned. What are these sounds of the mountain, announcing its own doom?

Yet still men go up into the mountains to see God, a God Who is most kind and merciful, a God Who is their Father while they are His children. They continue to climb these heights to gaze upon what they call the marvels of creation. Alas, where is kindness here, or mercy?

Comrades of my youth, we often set out together in the old days, and now you are fathers of families, even fathers of grown children, and have established your children in their professions and married off your daughters. Is it only through long-established habit that you still set forth today, confident and not despairing; that you still set forth in search of God and, as you watch the sunrise on some mountain peak four thousand meters high, find Him at last?

The God you seek is not in nature. Nature in no way expresses Him. What is it then that draws you to nature—despite the effort of rising from bed in the early hours and carrying a heavy knapsack and a heavy coil of rope and an ice-axe? What is this need which compels you to go where you can see nature spread out before you in all its primitive integrity? What could it be, if not the need of a greater fulfillment, of a greater stature for yourselves—a need which your education has led you to confound with the idea of the presence of God?

★

What does nature mean to communism? Does it even exist for communism? It is obvious that communism comes between man and nature, but how much of nature does it comprehend? What are its reactions? Does nature mean anything more to communism, for instance, than huge quantities of oil as yet unexploited, immense possibilities of hydraulic power still to be harnessed, or vast areas of wheat, wheat held simply as value for exchange? Is nature no more—in the eyes of communism—than a mine of untapped resources which must be transformed into useful riches, into riches for the state, into riches to be exchanged, turned into money, let us say into dollars and pounds, with which to buy machinery, or cannon, or airplanes, in the land of the dollar or the pound? Has such a preeminently poetic word, so great a word as "nature," now paled into a synonym for "raw materials"? Communism alone is not guilty; the entire world seems to have succumbed to this utilitarian madness. By thus degrading it, nature is made merely a source of potential energy to be ravaged by men through craft or violence. And to this violation nature must yield.

Nature, in other words everything, everything outside ourselves—earth, sea, and sky, animals, vegetables and minerals—lies open to exploitation, for man has to satisfy certain fundamental needs and these in turn produce an endless succession of other needs. "Infinite is man's concupiscence." Man is the pirate, driven by his greed to the unknown shores where nature's hidden gold awaits him. Helplessly nature awaits the predatory creature, watching him close in upon its shores, armed with new instruments which he discovered thanks to nature, but which, with sharp ingratitude, he uses to plunder it. Behold a mortal duel between man and nature! This is not too inaccurate a picture of how the Soviets look at it—although despite their cynicism, they would probably claim that they seek not only to master but to understand, since they too realize that nature, besides its riches, has many secrets. But here again, the Soviets ignore the power of love. For them there is only one way to understand—through science. They have created groups of scientists for what they call pure research without thought of profit, or at least of immediate profit. Pure scientists could be said to belong to the same family as contemplatives: like the contemplative, the research scientist seeks no profit; like the contemplative, he wants only to find a truth, to establish a fact which will give him a feeling of fulfillment because it reconciles something outside man to something within him, something in nature to something in man. Thus even the scientist (in his own way) can love. But love presupposes freedom—complete freedom (of course I mean inner freedom)—and one may well ask whether Soviet science does not lack this vital freedom, since communist scientists must relate facts only to their ideology, and not to the human soul. The exploitation of nature by Soviet science—an exploitation which is purely commercial, although entirely justifiable—might possibly be carried so far that it became subjective exploitation, deliberately made to serve prejudice and preconceived convictions, since communism is fundamentally hostile to the objective outer world.

Communism is primarily a kind of humanism, an excessive humanism, since it rejects everything outside man himself. To communism, man is both nothing and everything. He is nothing, since he dies; yet he is everything, since he is the chief preoccupation and everything else is judged only in relation to him and his material needs. Communism therefore can neither collaborate with nature nor trust it; communism must act the profiteer, the exploiting colonial, the conqueror just started on his path of conquest but on the verge of conquering more than he dreamed, and must encroach upon nature, encroach more and more, until (at the theoretical limit) nature ceases to exist, or is reduced to an abject slavery —which, for nature, would mean to exist no more.

I wonder if this is not the crucial point. For it is possible to dislike the socialist, communist, or materialist conception (call it what you will) of society and of man's rôle in society; you can raise innumerable objections to such more or less transitory aspects of its organization as forced labor and the dictatorship of the proletariat; but none of this can entirely explain the feeling of uneasiness that any contact with it rouses. You would do your best to accept the living conditions imposed by the system (you tell yourself); you would not refuse to work under official orders; you would even agree to being poorly fed, poorly housed, poorly clad, and to waiting in line at shops—but the uneasiness would still be there (for me, at least), obscure and vague and deep. What is this uneasiness? It takes some time to find out. But little by little you discover that it lies in the very depths of man, of your kind of man, since, in this matter, a man can speak only for himself. You discover that before all else you are a human being, and that it is precisely the human being in you whom communism is most anxious to stifle, for it cannot tolerate the human being. Whether consciously or not, communism can only tolerate man as a unit, and one man-unit is the same as another; it values man as a productive unit, it values his power to reason, but it absolutely never values his power for passion (with the exception of the single passion for the system itself).

The chief cause for uneasiness comes from having to accept a system the main characteristic of which is the curious absence of love, the lack of any kind of veneration (save love of itself and veneration of itself). You find yourself confronting a faith which you must accept in its entirety —or disappear. You find yourself face to face with an authoritarian religion which, through a strange irony, has no cult of anything but itself, a religion which condemns man to perpetual contemplation and admiration of himself—if not as he is, then as he will become; if not for his future accomplishments, then for the progressive development which will bring about his deification.

166

We all must adore something or someone; if we have nothing else, it is our own ego to which we bow. It is characteristic of this form of atheism that it makes man hostile to everything outside himself; in other words, it substitutes for an objective cult an entirely subjective cult which neither Christian, nor Mussulman, nor primitive Negro, nor ancient Greek, nor Buddhist ever knew, a cult which is not the fusion of man with something outside himself, but rather his total concentration upon himself. It is peculiar to communism (in the Russian form) to fix man's limitations, not beyond him, but strictly within him, so that all he can respect is his own development. After all, communism, this kind of communism, entails contempt for everything outside the system, for everything outside its special concept of man. And this concept of man sets communism against nature, for nature is here only an arena for man's future struggles—and since nature opposes man's efforts with inertia, he can win only by enslaving it.

The Greeks worshipped Zeus the Thunderer who represented the mystery hidden in the forces of nature; the Christians worshipped the source of this mystery. But the militant atheist, though he does not deny the existence of the

mystery, considers it only a product of man's
ignorance, a temporary obstacle to knowledge,
which will be counterbalanced by the sure advance of science and its final eradication of all
mystery. Hence what the atheist does not yet
know is an insult to what he already knows; what
he cannot yet do (what he is so far incapable of
doing) is a mockery of what he can do already. A
tacit struggle is therefore taking place between
man and all that surrounds him. He thinks that
his material surroundings are merely resources
to be tapped for his own needs, while he feels
that his spiritual surroundings are relentlessly
accusing him of intellectual inferiority.

A man of this sort never goes down on his
knees; he cannot go down on his knees; he is fundamentally ignorant of prayer. Here is perhaps
the crux of the matter: there are men who pray
and men who do not pray. I refer to all kinds of
praying, for there are a thousand ways to pray:
you can pray with words or without them; you
can pray in the name of a dogma or you can pray
without benefit of dogma; you can pray to some
one thing or some one person; or you can worship, as the African Negro does, a bush or a
mountain; or, like the pagans, you can worship
the mysterious underlying forces which bend the

bush or shatter the mountain; you can pray to
the gods, to all sorts of gods, or to the one God;
you can pray to Christ, or to the Saints. It is irrel-
evant (I mean in this argument) to what or to
whom you pray, for every prayer is an attempt to
enter into communion with something or someone outside ourselves to whom we grant objective
existence; to whom we even grant an existence
infinitely more important and mightier than our
own, and the existence of which we not only recognize, but venerate, precisely because it surpasses us—an existence upon which we therefore
bestow our love. But atheism loves only itself,
communes only with itself; apart from this self-
love and this egocentric communion it has nothing.

But you who are writing this, whom do you
love or what do you love, people may ask, and
what proofs of your love do you furnish? Is not
love of justice, the communists will ask, a valid
love? Were we not proving that at least we loved
justice when we ruined everything in order to
instate it? Is it not a proof of love for our fellow
men, or at least a way of showing love for our
fellow men, to seek justice for all mankind? Is it

not love for someone outside ourselves? And this "communion" of which you spoke, might it not be used simply to bind men to each other, men who are striving by common effort to master nature and thus gain a better way of life?

And so I apologize for using so great a word (the word "love") and one so difficult to define; but there is no way of avoiding it. After all, does not the whole problem come down to this: that some men can only love a limited number of things, while others cannot love at all unless they love everything? Perhaps there is a restricted love, valid and sufficient for such men as, say, the communists, and also an all-embracing love which alone would satisfy other men. To these others, love is impossible unless it is universal love. These are the Christians, or to be more exact, the religious spirits. They can love only through the love of God; for them, love is charity (in the Christian sense of the word). But, for the communists, for the atheists, love is always for one thing as against another, one thing opposed to another, and they can only love man by denying all that exceeds his powers. The Christian finds his stature through trust, through his complete trust in everything and through his common bonds (*religio*) with all that exists outside

170

himself, infinitely beyond him in quantity and
size, but giving him, in quality, because he trusts
it, his true spiritual place. On the other hand, the
atheist must isolate himself, learn to know himself and make a concrete place for himself by a
continual effort to invent machines, by a continual struggle to master all-important matter and
so establish a stature not for one individual, but
for the masses, since he believes only in humanity in the mass, a humanity steadily increasing
its powers through new discoveries and thus creating a treasure in which each individual has the
inalienable right to an abstract share, though it
belongs to none. All humanity, therefore, raises
its stature—in a void and for a brief moment. At
the same time humanity feels nothing but contempt for nature, while constantly making as
many inroads upon it as possible. For this communist humanity does not, and cannot possibly,
love nature.

Communist humanity loves itself. It loves itself all the more because it has nothing else to
love. That is why we are witnessing a strange
phenomenon in Russia today: not, as one might
suppose, the disappearance of faith (there is far

greater fervor in Russia than in the other nations of Europe) but the direct opposite to disappearance of faith—in other words, the intensifying of faith in another direction. Communism has not tried to repress faith; it has given it a new objective, a wholly materialistic objective. But you must have blind faith in that objective, since it is not visible, at least not yet. You must have faith, and you either have it or not. You must believe in the new man, the man of tomorrow, the regenerated man, redeemed (by his own efforts). It is clear that we are dealing here with a true messianism without a Messiah—and its fulfillment depends not on a god but on mankind. So it is essential for mankind to believe in this messianism and all mankind must be converted. Communism is a church and a remarkably authoritarian church. The Soviets have substituted for the ancient religions a new one, or if you prefer, a parody. There are Soviet altars, Soviet Saints, Soviet rituals and a Soviet symbolism. There have been and will be Soviet Popes and Soviet Councils. There are Soviet processions. The Soviets have their Mass; the Soviet religion has its witnesses and martyrs. Communism, the word itself, has no meaning, save by virtue of a common faith. "You have no tenderness, you have only justice, and therefore you are unjust," says Dostoevsky. Tenderness is total love, whereas justice is only a part of love, though it believes itself, mistakenly, to be the whole. The part thinks it is the whole and imitates the whole, but since it can never be more than a part, its new religion is merely a parody.

This Soviet faith condemns man to emptiness, to the void envisaged by communist religion as man's final fate, a void from which we all emerged and into which we shall be plunged back again. But the communists must make every effort to blunt man's awareness of this void because of the effect upon him that such a discovery might have. Their religion must stupefy or intoxicate man with relentless activity and so prevent him from feeling or thinking for himself. It must rouse him with blaring bands and harangue him with speeches, arguments, tracts and posters to force him to think only in terms of collectivity. The word "church," in the strictly human and worldly sense (if it is ever permissible to use it thus), has never been more fittingly applied than to daily life in the Soviet State. There is a most obvious and exact parallel between the real Church and the Soviet State, and between their organizations; both the Church and the Soviet State have dogmas; both have a principle of au-

173

thority; both have a clergy, both have their faithful—and specially dedicated groups to watch over their salvation. There is only one difference: in the Soviet State, God has been replaced by mankind. The worship of an immutable God has been replaced by the worship of human progress and prayer has been replaced by work. Work has been made holy. Man must still attain salvation by his own efforts, but with this difference, that he need no longer attain it through a relationship with God, but exclusively through a relationship with his fellow-men, in which he makes the maximum effort to increase the resources of collective mankind.

Communism also has in common with the Catholic Church the principle of universality: for it cannot consider itself universally true until it has conquered the whole world from pole to pole and linked east to west through the Equator. It is also like the Church because, although it confines its aims to man's earthly life, it claims to achieve his transformation, or rather, his transfiguration: it claims that it can take man as he is, in his infinite variety, and mould him in a single shape.

Despite his efforts, however, man is still not entirely detached from nature for nature still works in him without his knowledge. Man is not wholly a conscious being: most of his organs function without his even being conscious of them. No matter how civilized, no matter how cultivated he may be, he still lives primarily through his reflexes. These processes of the body are hidden, and, because of their mystery and their kinship with the great forces of nature, man has long thought of them as sacred. It was always considered a sin to interfere with the secret processes of the body, even when this was possible; there was nothing to do but submit for man was subject to elemental laws, doubtless of divine origin, which he had no right to oppose. In rejecting God, the Soviets also rejected the feeling of respect; especially respect for nature. This lack of respect for nature fosters a profound cynicism. While their attitude toward hygiene, which is part of the battle against sickness, seems legitimate enough, part of this battle is waged against fertility, which they take upon themselves to regulate—along with everything else—simply because they are able to do so. All the mysteries in fertility, still hidden even from the scrutiny of the scientist, cannot restrain them

when they discover that they can control fertility
—if only empirically. They are not held back for
a single instant by the thought that they cannot
see far ahead in this direction and that their interference not only qualifies a basic reality within
their grasp but also qualifies the consequences
which they can only dimly foresee, and even
qualifies the consequences of these consequences,
which elude them entirely. They are motivated
by hatred of the divine masked by an ideal of
utility, for they are in rivalry with God, or with
the idea of God. They are actually jealous, which
is somewhat comic. Their interference grows all
the bolder the more deeply they feel the mystery,
for the mystery exacerbates them since it may be
concealing God. And so it is with a kind of fury
that they attack the sources of life itself by the
open, official, "hygienic" practice of abortion.
Moreover, if it were possible for man to deter-
mine sex in advance and to select sex in advance,
they would doubtless do this also. To oppose
nature everywhere for utilitarian reasons is certainly what prompts their actions, their reckless
actions, but are they really prompted only by util-
itarianism? A Catholic would be more likely to
consider their actions Satanic, inspired by a certain delight in destroying the things in nature

176

which are not of human origin, a task, the Catholic would add, beyond man's power without the Devil's aid. It is ironic to note that the Soviets have not yet dared to carry out the logical sequence of their principles, for you do not yet see them killing the aged, the infirm, the incurable, in other words, the useless; but perhaps they will come to that. At present, their lack of respect for life (through a strange contradiction) has apparently stopped short at the threshold of consciousness. But how can you establish limits to the concept of usefulness if it is not counter-balanced by anything else? The Soviets must be sorely tempted to go still further because the legal murder which they so far practice only on the unconscious embryonic child could be perpetrated upon conscious human beings in the most scientific, or the most humanitarian manner—in other words, painlessly; and for the wholehearted devotee of hygiene it is pain alone that counts and not the destruction of life.

The chief effort of the atheistic communists—we must repeat—is to shift man from existence on a twofold plane, the divine and the earthly, to existence on a single plane, by which I mean to narrow him down from a universal love to love for one thing alone. Yet atheism is still forced to uphold the principle of universality within its declared limitations; it is compelled, if only to avoid confusion, to impose its ideology on all men alike and to make it the universal bedrock of society. Since it is impossible to reconcile extreme opposites, and difficult even to reconcile differences, it is essential to try to make men alike. Article One in the atheist program is the obliteration of all differences.

Everyone knows how Russian communism has enforced uniformity—by the so-called dictatorship of the proletariat. The dictatorship of the proletariat, however, is only a strategy: the domination of one class is to be temporary, according to the doctrine, and must eventually lead to the abolition of classes. And these classes themselves (these differences) according to the doctrine, are merely arbitrary. It is interesting to note that, in the matter of social classes, the Soviets claim to be in accord with the law of nature, at least theoretically, since they place the responsibility for class distinctions upon society alone.

Yet we must look further into this question, from the materialist point of view. Materialism calls itself dynamic, it sees itself only in motion;

materialism never stakes its claims on today, but is always ready to seek justification in tomorrow: it completely adheres to the directives which it calls its permanent line. Let us observe how this communist line shapes the individual, or will shape him; how it already has shaped him. You can easily see that, for the communists, the ideal man is the closest to a standard type (to use a standard industrial term). If one man is equal to another, one individual to the next, there can be units of men — interchangeable units — with which to build. Moreover this standard man is, from the materialist viewpoint, a physiological entity. Materialism, a certain kind of materialism, finds it impossible to avoid physiological premises; so, too, does communist theory. That men look alike, that there is human equality, confirms for Christians their belief in a divine origin, since man is made in God's image, but the communists only see in man's equality a fact. For example, man's height varies relatively little and if his weight varies more, it is because he eats too much or not enough—the result of a faulty system of distribution. Everywhere man has the same function; he has the same material needs— the only needs that are real—and these roughly constitute one single need, the need for physical

179

survival. In other words, what man needs most is nourishment, or in more scientific language, a certain number of calories.

Thus materialism bases its society upon a wholly abstract type of man, the "standard" man whose stature has been reduced to his quantitative value, who represents only that one value, and whose likeness to other men is based only on that one value: a man, then, who is entirely contrary to nature. For although this concept of man conforms to nature in one certain aspect, the doctrine itself is contrary to nature since it only accounts for this one aspect of man. Nature enjoys variety and likes to induce variety by bringing into play her many different facets: air, water, plants, soil of different kinds, and different climates; and it is possible to imagine a philosophy or a sociology inspired by nature and eager to further this natural diversity in man. But communist materialism, we are obliged once again to point out, is always motivated by hatred of nature (if by nature we mean everything outside man) because nature somehow refuses to submit; it cannot be forced to yield entirely to man. Materialism therefore tries its utmost to eradicate whatever in man brings man close to nature, such as his use of his hands, his use of tools. Materialism, born of machinery, calls on machinery to do man's work. It has based all its society on the machine; by every possible means it is increasing the use of the machine. Here we must note that the use of the machine is also ideological and that Russian communism did not adopt the "machine age" of capitalism out of purely utilitarian considerations. The chief characteristic of the machine is that it gives man a *force* which, at its theoretical limit, would free him completely from physical effort and demand no more than his presence, a kind of spiritual presence (if "spiritual" is not too strong a word). The machine eliminates man's direct contact with matter, a contact which is somewhat of a drain on his strength, but at the same time converts it, by fusing the muscles with the will, thus enabling him to impose himself on matter not only with his body but also with his mind. A tool is a kind of hand, harder or sharper, with a greater reach or grasp; it is an extended arm, or both arms, or the arms and legs together; in other words, the tool is man's body, for it is his body which governs and moves the tool. Tools offer continual resistance; man is continually forced to overcome that resistance. He reacts in many different ways to this effort *and these reactions are embodied in his work.* For he can be happy or unhappy, satisfied by what he makes or dissatisfied; he can be either inspired (for there is inspiration even in manual labor), or devoid of inspiration; and his work is like a barometer which registers the play of the emotions. Through tools he is intimately involved with nature, continually taught by nature; and this is precisely what the Soviets most hate. They see that the machine not only eliminates direct contact but cuts the current, a certain life-current, flowing from matter to man. The Soviets want to reverse this current and make it flow from man to matter. They will go on installing machinery everywhere because it helps them to create the only kind of man they want. They founded their régime on the proletariat, on the factory worker—in other words, on a worker who is a kind of mechanic. They will make everyone a mechanic—for they see, thanks to the United States and to the bourgeois world in general, that this is not only possible in the future, but already possible now.

Logically, therefore, their first step will be to liquidate the peasant. Within measure, the bourgeois world has allowed, and still allows, the peasant to exist, though his existence in most of our European countries, dependent on protective tariffs and state premiums, has become extraordinarily artificial. The bourgeois world found itself unable, in the face of its liberalism, to impose overnight upon collective mankind the social measures which its technical progress seemed to demand. But the Soviets, who inherited this progress from the bourgeois world, are not bound by the same scruples; they are sworn, on the contrary, to an active propaganda, to a sustained war against "natural" man—the man who, wherever he clings to his last ramparts, is still acquiring wisdom from nature.

★

Fundamentally, Soviet humanism sees the universe only as a vast sum of quantities and therefore has no love for the universe. One can love quality, but not quantity. And since nature in itself is only a sum of quantities, Soviet humanism does not love nature. Nature is actually an enemy, since it hems man in on all sides and opposes its inertia to his will. To Soviet humanism, nature is only an empty space on the map for mankind to colonize. That humanity can occupy and exploit this empty space is not only possible but probable and even certain; since it has the weapons of science, is still in its early youth, having come into existence in relatively recent times, and is infinitely capable of perfectibility. The ultimate mysteries, variously named, but worshipped in the past by men of all religions and still held sacred by many, merely represent—for the Soviets—the unknown, that is, what is now unknown but will sooner or later be divulged. Obviously there is no reason to worship the unknown, or respect it, or fear it, or pray to it; all we need do is to study it scientifically, through analysis and experiment. This attitude toward the universe is indeed a cold one; nor does it quite face reality. For the great expectation of discovery may be an illusion. The future is supposed to supply the answers; but the future might not supply them at all. At the same time, however, we are told that we must have faith in the future. Communist materialism, we repeat, is based on faith, faith in a future which remains entirely undefined and can be indefinitely postponed, but a future which must make perfect a present necessarily imperfect and incomplete.

This form of humanism is said to be purely materialistic, and no doubt it is, and deliberately so, but for my part I would be sorely tempted to blame it for not being materialistic enough. It relies entirely on the concept of inert matter, in other words on a concept of matter which science abandoned more than thirty years ago.

At that time the atom was believed to be stable, motionless; therefore chemistry was the first of the sciences. But chemistry was only interested in the molecule. Actually there first came the human mind which was quick with motion and could quicken, and what it quickened was matter. It was because man believed matter to be inert that he could also believe that he controlled its manifestations. It was on the premise of inert matter that materialism based its belief in the permanence and inviolability of scientific laws and therefore in the philosophy of determinism. Could Marx be obsolete now, together with his theories and all their interpretations?

For now, suddenly, we have the atom to look at, I mean for the scientists to look at. Not only can the atom be split, but it is also capable of motion, unstable, and, in its infinite smallness, infinitely great, since it contains, within itself, the same relationships of measure and speed that we find in the stars. We now know that the atom also has its laws—and they are not at all the laws we attribute to lifeless matter. For the atom has suddenly proved to be alive. We observe its life with wide-eyed surprise, with startled minds, but our spirit marvels at the atom and loves it for in its life we recognize a likeness to our own. Once again, therefore, man's spirit faces the deepest mystery—just where we thought that none existed; and, discovering suddenly that a likeness exists between all the elements of matter, we even see, in this farthest advance of scientific research, that there is also a likeness between all these elements and ourselves. For what are the electric particles in the atom? To the scientist, they do not seem to have either mass or dimension. Then what are they? Are they spirit? It is their union and their cohesion which give matter its mass and dimension: the thing without mass creates mass; the thing without dimension creates dimension. How? Why? Could it be that spirit creates matter? Could it be that spirit conceives matter through the act of coming together, through the coupling of seminal elements which appear to obey, as we ourselves obey, the phenomena of attraction and repulsion, and yield, as we yield ourselves, to the law of love? Is it no more than poetic exaltation to say that matter is rooted in love? How far we are removed from Marxism!

I have suggested that Marxism may be outdated and I assure the reader that this is not because I care so much about being up-to-date myself, for I am well aware how trivial that is and I know the risks you run when you try to be in fashion. Nor would I dream of reproaching Marx and his disciples for having wanted to be up-to-date in their times. The fact remains, however, that Marx had scientific ambitions and claimed to apply to his own "science"—the science of man —only the best scientific methods. He may have to pay heavily for this. For science goes its way, heedless of the effect of its discoveries upon society. Science puts up a framework of truth today, but tomorrow it might be compelled to tear it down—nor will it hesitate to do so. Meanwhile man goes on living. Unlike science, man does not live wholly on hypothesis and experiment. He lives with all his being: not only in mind but in body too, and in passion and in need. How could man let his whole life depend on some scientific concept which, precisely because it is scientific, must surely change? Man longs for permanence, he wants above all else to endure. Man seems to have been created for one single purpose: to go on living, to go on pouring his own creation into the sum of all things created.

Marxist materialism is a partial philosophy because it deals only with certain parts of the truth, or more exactly, with only one part of the truth.

Marxism does not simplify so much as over-simplify, for simplification consists in harmonizing the jarring elements of a problem, while over-simplification ignores whatever elements it cannot reconcile. For instance, Marxism believes in "continual progress," which is certainly a simplification but an arbitrary one, for how is it possible not to see that nothing is gained in life without a simultaneous loss, that every gain is forthwith matched by a loss—in other words, that every gain has a price? Specifically, how is it possible not to see that the substitution of the machine for the tool—a major Marxist victory (though man's "final liberation," to be brought about by the machine, is prudently relegated by Marxism to the future)—is simply a substitution of one process for another and that while man may indeed obtain certain advantages from it some day, for the moment the disadvantages are obvious.

MAN AND LABOR

W HEN YOU look down, you do not see anyone. But you know that there are workers in the vineyards; and further along the lake shore, there are lawyers, or street cleaners, there are clerks at their desks, and still further along there are peasants, and beyond there are men who live high up in the mountain valleys while on the other side there are men at work in the vineyards again, or employees, laborers, ministers, professors, civil servants. They have little to worry them; they have enough to live on. They come and go from their houses to their vineyards or their fields, to their offices or workshops. They have little to worry them; many have a bit of land of their own. They have some money in the savings bank; almost all are comfortably clothed and cleanly housed.

Even the railroad worker, beneath this sky empty of complaints, lives in a small, neat brick house with a garden and a plot of vegetables. You would only have to walk a few steps to see his home along the railroad tracks, not far from where the track comes out of the tunnel. The railroad worker has taken off his cap, the blue smock he wears as a uniform, and the jacket he wears underneath the smock, and having hung them on a fence-stake, he has begun to spade the earth in his garden. From time to time he stops, stands up, and lights his pipe. He is not unhappy. Must he be made unhappy?

He must be made unhappy, say the revolutionaries. If the proletarian is happy, it is because he has no needs: he must be made to have needs. If those who have nothing are content with their lot, it is because they can imagine no other lot: they must be made to see that they could have a different lot, if only they felt the need of it. They must be given needs which they cannot satisfy. People who still use oil-lamps must be made envious of those who have electric light; a family of five confined in a single room must be made to resent the fact that a well-off couple has a whole house to itself; and the woman who goes to the fountain to draw water must be made discontented by the fact that her neighbor has water running from a tap. Material needs must be created first, and from these in due time will be born spiritual needs, so that all men may have an equal chance to fulfill themselves, starting always from the same point, no longer sadly handicapped, as they are for the most part today, by circumstances. The problem is therefore to change these circumstances by an inflationary process, so to speak—in other words, to make universal needs which are now quite rare.

Revolution is based on discontent, on an artificially stimulated discontent. Revolution also depends on hatred, for you must come to believe that what you lack and others have has been stolen from you.

The proletarian is a man who has been dispossessed; the proletarian turns into a revolutionary as soon as he becomes conscious of this fact.

It is a far more serious matter than most privileged people realize: for these men who have been dispossessed and possess nothing will see to it that the privileged are dispossessed in turn; they have had the privileged over them and now they will turn this order upside down; they have been oppressed and now they will find compensation in oppressing—until economic equality has at last been established, and then there will be no more classes (at least according to the revolutionaries).

This viewpoint denies all metaphysics and is therefore directly opposed to the Christian, metaphysical viewpoint—for it asserts that there is nothing *afterward—meta:* afterward. They deny the afterward, these revolutionaries, so their hatred is especially frightening; they love man for himself and in himself, but they do not love him in God. The Christian can hate the evil in man and yet love man himself, for he loves man in God; but the hatred of the materialist, for whom there is no God, comprises not only man's guilt but the whole of him. The materialist does not love his neighbor as himself, but only as his neighbor agrees with him. To the materialist there is no such thing as sin, nor any way of judging man apart from his guilt; a man's guilt is the whole man, even when that guilt consists only in being different. The hatred of the revolutionary is implacable; on this point the bourgeois are not mistaken. Revolutionaries have an excuse for hatred: they are making a desperate effort—the effort of men who no longer believe in anything except the effort itself. We have come to see that man can count only on himself. The men who have nothing, and these are the great majority, are told: "Look, you have nothing"; then they are told: "Look, you can have everything."

For the world has a future, but it is only through the united, active participation of all men that this future can be realized.

We must be fair: at present the bourgeoisie is right when it says that communism is *founded in hatred,* but communism is also right in saying that this hatred is in the name of justice. Communism, of course, begins by exploiting the anger of humiliated men, but only as a tactical move. It can argue that hatred is merely the reverse side of love. It can argue, moreover, that its hatred for the way things are is all the greater because of its love for the way things could be, and that, in the last analysis, it hates the present only in the light of the future. The hatred which communism rouses for purposes of its own is only a tool borrowed from the grim reality of today, and one to be cast aside, it hopes, before too long. And if you challenge communism for its purely materialist outlook, it will answer that of course it is materialist, since it believes in matter; but that it also acknowledges higher degrees of matter and that these are precisely what other people, the bourgeois, call spiritual.

One must begin, therefore, by breeding discontent among those who have nothing. One must stir a longing for air and light in those who lack air and light; one must stir a longing for cleanliness in those who live in filth, a longing for decent clothes in those who wear rags, a longing for enough to eat in those who go hungry.

Most men lack imagination; they do not see that there might be nothing at all. They do not even see that things might be different. They do not look for potentialities beyond what they can see. They must be made to see these potentialities and to realize that fulfillment is up to them.

This is the reverse of Christian doctrine which tells you to be content with what you have, since there will be compensation elsewhere. Communism, on the other hand, tells you that there is neither a compensation, nor an elsewhere.

This is the true humanism, the belief that there is nothing beyond man and that "man" no longer connotes—as it used to—a handful of privileged men; but that it now means all mankind, that the problem is to see that all men become privileged, and especially that all men be made "gifted," since the gifted human being is not simply a product of nature but a product of society as well.

Man must first be made unhappy, both because of what he has not yet got and also because of what he has not yet become. Men must be made ashamed of their inertia and their sloth, for they are to emancipate all the unborn. This, too, may be a kind of grandeur.

★

To the peasant, to the worker in the vineyard, and also to the laborer, people preach the coming of a new world in which money will no longer count; I mean a world in which it may still be possible to have money, but there will be no point in having it, since the focal point of life will have changed and man's chief preoccupation, no matter what his trade, will no longer be to build up his fortune or resources, but to express himself fully through his work, through all kinds of work.

There is to be a world where the advantages of life will no longer be bought by money, but by merit. In other words, by giving yourself, you will gain the world, and that is a noble concept.

But this new world must be taken on faith at first because it does not yet exist and it is only through faith that the day may come when it will exist. What communism offers mankind—communism at its most noble and pure (obviously, I do not refer to its immediate political and economic plans)—is a kind of heroism.

To Christian mythology communism now opposes the myth of Hercules: it combats the hydra, pursues the wild boar. Christianity is based on resignation; while communism, which is a form of integral humanism, refuses resignation. Humanism, born in fifteenth-century Italy, is only now reaching its full development. Since each new idea is conditioned by time, there is a long lapse before it can be fully realized; it is only little by little that it frees itself from the past and enters the future to which it belongs. For a long time man, who had abandoned God, lived on with God unconsciously, no longer worshipping Him but tolerating Him. The idea, the new idea, expresses itself at first within the framework of a ritual which excludes it. It does not break abruptly with ways established long before it appeared. At first, the new idea is not even clearly aware of the consequences it entails. Then comes a revolution, and then another, and they attempt to lay bare the idea and then transmute it into fact.

Inherent in humanism is the primacy of man. In this connection, let us not forget how laboriously man has made his way down the centuries to our times, how patiently and with what tireless effort he has tried to change himself. For ages he held second place and accepted his second place:

but today, man comes first. Early humanism was exclusively concerned with an élite: it is only now that it embraces all mankind. At first humanism was aristocratic: humanism provided for the few, for the "best" (and there was religion for the masses). At first, humanism only offered its opportunities, both material and spiritual, to a small minority; now, however, it sees that its task is to offer these opportunities to everyone, for now it is convinced that all men have equal rights and equal rights to everything. This is the primacy of man. Man comes first. There is no God above him. Either God commands or man commands. Either God assigns man his rôle in this world through revelation, and then God is the master and man takes his authority from God; or else man is alone and it is for him to succeed in deciphering the message which is confined entirely to this world. Then man is his own master, and when he has deciphered and spelled out the world, he will have conquered it.

There is no middle way. The middle ways, the compromises by which we live, are only makeshifts. They are prompted by the needs of the human heart, needs which man cannot quite deny even when he is convinced that he lives by reason alone. Man does not easily relinquish his forebears; drawn to the future, he is yet held back by the past. He is twofold, for he is himself, and at the same time he is all who have preceded him. He is confused and complex, consisting as he does of sundry contradictions which, more often than not, he can only reconcile by lies and self-deceit. He is forever diffused, forever tormented by a longing for integration. Thus every man, in his innate diffusion, represents the various stages of mankind throughout the centuries: where mankind came from, but also where mankind is going; the starting point, but also the goal—and either both are God, or neither are God, with whatever variations you want on this central theme.

But perhaps the atheist lacks imagination. Have the atheists carried out their ideas to the logical conclusion? For without God man is inevitably ephemeral in an ephemeral world. Man without God is impermanent in an impermanent world. Yet he is not only asked to make the best of this impermanence, but even told to be proud of it. He must build, knowing that all he builds will be destroyed, knowing that nothing lasts, knowing that neither he himself nor what he creates will last. This is why he takes refuge in the idea of society. He renounces his own existence and transfers his private hopes to the collective hopes of mankind. If he achieves any progress, it is only a fraction, for real progress must be made by mankind as a whole. And there is also the fact of death for him to face. He must reconcile himself to his death by accepting the idea that, in reproducing himself, he attains a certain kind of immortality, an immortality for mankind—or if not strictly speaking an immortality, at least a sufficiently long lease on life to make the effort worthwhile.

Those who are satisfied with the idea of relativity say "a million years," and believe that they have said all that needs to be said.

Yet are they not looking at things somewhat too narrowly? Are they not using too small a scale? They count up to a million—a high number—and believe that they have said all that needs to be said.

But add millions to millions and still you have nothing, because it is only a part, and a part is nothing, if you have not the whole.

★

The Christian said: "Man has to suffer, for suffering is the fruit of original sin." Marxism maintains that there is no such thing as original

201

sin. Indeed this denial is basic in its doctrine. While eighteenth-century philosophy said: "Man is born naturally good," Marxism says: "Man is born neither good nor bad; man is born of chance; man is an amalgam of potentialities from which one must extract those best fitted to a doctrine. We Marxists have a doctrine: we need only apply it."

"We shall cultivate man as we cultivate the plants," say the Marxists. "We shall correct his errors (though there are no errors, and there can be no correction of errors without fixed principles by which to judge). When you talk about inevitable suffering, what do you mean? Is poverty, for instance, inevitable? We are putting an end to poverty by putting an end to private property. Is disease inevitable? Science is winning its battle against disease, for disease does not come from God. In most cases disease is caused by the failings of society: for example, consider how the industrial system forces the factory worker to live; consider the run-down, cramped houses, the promiscuity engendered by greed; consider those slums without air, light, or running water, where so many men, women and children eke out a hopeless existence. Wherever you look you see that the circumstances imposed by society (circumstances which we are now changing completely) are the source of most physical ills. We believe that man is his own master and therefore that he alone is responsible for mankind. It is up to mankind to tend and cure itself. We shall put disease in its place—a very small place—for perhaps disease is only inevitable and 'natural' to the extent that we make room for it. The word 'natural' means unavoidable: we may eventually be able to prove that nothing is unavoidable, or at least that death alone is unavoidable and 'natural' (for the time being, until further notice).

"And what is it that makes death an evil? It is our fear of death. What is it that makes us consider death so great a calamity? It is our constant foreboding. We fear death because, in a capitalistic society where man is only concerned with himself and his family, and cares only for himself and his family, death is the chief threat.

"Man is like the leaf of the ivy which yellows and falls without heeding the season, but we communists say that only the ivy plant itself is important; that it has many leaves and although they fall one after another, as fast as they fall they are replaced, they even increase in number, and therefore the ivy plant endures and survives all seasons. The leaf must be made aware of its

rôle: it must abandon the idea that it can be both
root and stem as well. Man is a mere fragment of
the all-important human society; he must think
only of the grandeur of collective humanity. Dedicated to this ideal, and in self-oblivion, he will
find the cure for all his ills; he will find his salvation. Most of the evils from which he suffers are
either curable or imaginary. We shall cure what
can be cured, and we shall banish the chimera of
man's fears by giving him a mighty task to accomplish."

Thus it is nothing short of a millenium which
Marxism—or at least one form of Marxism—offers: the overthrow of false values and the substitution of true values—in short a paradise, entirely earthly to be sure, but a veritable paradise.
Marxism is the image in reverse of Christian
hopes; it situates in this life what the Christian
placed in Heaven. The enemy of Christianity
hopes some day to win, despite nature and his
own limitations, a paradise made to his measure,
manufactured, mechanically manufactured by
himself. This paradise does not yet exist but it is
going to exist and that is why there must be faith
in it. But Marxism offers no proof that this still
remote new life will surely come: it is unable to
give any positive proof. The first steps to bring

this paradise into existence prove nothing yet, nor do the setbacks it has suffered. The setbacks are unavoidable, the partial achievements without significance. Marxism needs much more time. It will have to carry its revolution beyond the borders of Russia before its achievements can offer conclusive proof. Meanwhile it lives by faith and hope—but for charity it has substituted solidarity, since it rejects love, and therein lies perhaps its greatest weakness. Man must believe in the Marxist paradise or at least in the mirage of this paradise. But man today is inordinately tired, extraordinarily weary of what he is and what he has; perhaps that weariness, that disgust, will suffice in itself to make him turn abruptly toward something *new*, especially when this something new seems within reach (since it is actually being tried out, for whatever it is worth, in Russia).

For all these reasons, humanity, eager to escape from a world apparently exhausted, may perhaps give itself up to the experiment. I think this is most likely to happen. But I do not see the outcome. Perhaps I lack faith. Total destruction obviously offers an opportunity to build up something entirely new; but there is no guarantee that the new edifice will be better than the old.

Now the great question arises: can man change himself? Or can he only combine anew the elements within him—those various elements which, although they remain constant, may, through an almost infinite number of combinations, take on many different aspects and sometimes give the appearance of being completely new? Where are the limits to what we call progress? To put it another way, going back to the question under discussion, how long will nature continue to tolerate man's interference?

The experiment has just begun: we can see and count the forces we have wrested from nature, but we cannot yet be sure that nature will not some day turn them against us. We succeed in curing many diseases; but are we not at the same time bringing others into existence? These great forces drawn from nature are as indifferent to evil as they are to good—to what we call evil and good—and they can work either for or against us, indiscriminately. Shall we ever master them sufficiently to make sure that they always move in the right direction? Need we never fear a violent reaction? Supposing there were two sides, with nature on the right and man on the left: could we say that it is possible to keep moving indefinitely in a straight line toward the left? Or could the moment come when the line curved back toward its point of origin? Does the straight line exist in nature? Every social or political system, every abstract plan ends by colliding with nature—that is, with nature itself or with the nature of man. Perhaps we shall have to learn that man does not go where he wills. Nature, and man too, are infinitely plastic, yet they have a stubborn resilience, a coiled, hidden spring which rebounds when pressed down to the limit.

Perhaps we are not enough aware of the process of continual counterbalance in life, whereby every gain is offset with a loss, every advance with a backward step. Perhaps we do not see clearly enough that we are clinging to a kind of knotted rope and how, as we pull ourselves up from one notch to the next, the rope itself is meanwhile being lowered exactly as far as we thought to have risen. We think that we are climbing; we stay where we are. No doubt man can go against nature for a long time. Nature appears to give man free rein, saying nothing; and man thinks he has conquered because nature makes no retort. Man thinks that he has enslaved nature to his ideologies; despite man's seeming triumph, however, nature is actually the victor. For we have famine, we have privations; we have political and civil war, we have disorder—here, there, and everywhere; it is becoming impossible to live. Man is at the point where he must either consent to his own destruction or, by a sudden change of mind, decide to admit the existence of needs he formerly denied.

Nature is long-suffering; its victory, quiet and unproclaimed. We do not realize at once how deeply nature is involved in the struggle; we do not recognize at once the link between our catastrophes and nature's rebellion. Nature works in shadow, unobtrusively, with a bitter gentleness, until its profound resistance causes a sudden outburst of catastrophe.

Can man exist without love? No doubt he can, for a time. But will he be able to exist without love forever?

Can man exist without worship, without the belief in something or someone beyond himself?

Can science alone fulfill all the needs of society?

Can man live forever on one single plane, the plane of the world he knows?

Is there not a human "capital" compounded of emotion, profoundly natural emotion, which, if neglected, will demand to be used?

Is there not a human "capital" of the imagination, also profoundly natural, which must invest itself in something?

Surely it is a fine thing to attack money, since money is one more inequality, and the least justifiable of them all. But it should be perfectly obvious that money is not the only value we inherit.

We are born unequal in the heart of social equality; this inequality and this equality will have to be reconciled. We are born tall or not tall, handsome or not handsome, strong or not strong. No one denies this, nor can anyone possibly deny it despite all future eugenics. We are born with various gifts, some physical, some not physical, and these it is society's function to employ.

If we are going to tear down everything in order to rediscover human nature, then it is *the whole* of human nature which we must discover.

Our method has been to turn our values upside down, yet the fact remains that *all* our values will have to be reestablished in their rightful places.

★

Admitting that a materialistic education can be set to work to mold man from the day of his birth (as in Russia now), you would still have to find out whether it can change him so completely that certain needs—needs which have seemed essential to him since his earliest history—will vanish without trace. This is the experiment now being undertaken in Russia and it is intensely interesting. I may add that it is not an experiment which can be brought to a conclusion overnight; neither we, nor our children, will live to know the results. But they have begun to work on it over there in the Russias, and it is more than just a beginning, for their whole society is obviously organized to isolate the child from metaphysical, or rather religious, influences considered harmful to its development.

Man has always believed in the supernatural: will he cease to believe in it, simply because no one speaks of it to him any more? Man has always been a religious creature: will he cease to be religious, when he learns or is taught that all religion is based on a lie? I do not have to be reminded that in our modern societies, even those which are capitalistic, religion is no longer universally accepted and that nowadays only a few have a truly living faith. Nevertheless religion still acts upon our society; it is in the atmosphere of our times, misty perhaps, yet pervasive, and the weak, the anxious, the unhappy, are exposed

to its influence. It is therefore imperative to get
down to the roots of the disease. That is what
they are trying to do in Russia; with the churches
gone, with all family influence removed, the only
contact allowed the child is his teachers, who
speak, of course, for the State. Will man, in these
circumstances, find a new religion, all by himself
and within himself—I mean some religion beyond materialism? Or if his need of the two
planes on which he used to live—the plane of
this world, the plane of the other world—is an
entirely artificial need (since it does not exist in
nature), will he learn to be satisfied with what
the materialists offer him—a life based exclusively on reason and negation of the supernatural? It is possible: man may be about to enter
an era in which he will feel no need beyond scientific knowledge.

This would be the real revolution, the only
conclusive revolution. For what we loosely call
revolutions should and do affect social conditions, but they can only permanently transform
the world when they touch man's inmost self,
when they change not only his outward appearance or his daily life, but his secret being and the
life of his spirit. We must find out whether it is
only the combinations (however numerous they

are) of irreducible elements in man which change, or whether these elements themselves are capable of change, in other words, whether or not man as we have known him remains eternally the same.

The man of the Left does not believe in "eternal" man (as the bourgeois call him). The man of the Left believes in unlimited progress. This idea that an increase need not be counterbalanced by a loss, this idea that there can be a net profit and a continual gain, is basic in his thinking. But it is exactly the opposite of the Christian idea or of any theory assuming that there can be no gain without loss, no progress without a backward step; it is the opposite of any theory denying the omnipotence of man and therefore compelled, in order to explain his relative impotence, to go back to the idea of a "fall" or of some insuperable obstacle which man must forever face. Man needs to live fully with every part of his being: body, heart, and mind. It remains to be seen whether he can live fully on one plane alone. Can he find complete fulfillment in his own potentialities, in a progressive and gradual mastery of matter? Or can this plenitude only be reached through the concept of cooperation with something outside himself, the concept of fusing his efforts with powers infinitely beyond his own; powers which, moreover, he can only use if they deign to come to his assistance? Faced with the contradictions and imperfections in his own nature, man has thought until now that he had something corrupt within him, or at least something still incomplete, which his own strength alone could never overcome.

But the man of the Left believes that there is a remedy for this humiliation and that the remedy can be found in his own future. The Right believes in the fixed and eternal; the Left believes in development and change. The Left believes that the man of today will be completed and redeemed by the man of tomorrow. Baudelaire defined civilization (I quote from memory) as "the gradual waning of the traces of original sin." Obviously Baudelaire belongs to the Right; his use of the word "waning" is negative. But the man of the Left, who owes it to himself to provide a positive definition, speaks of a "growing" good. And since he admits no limits to this growth, there is no reason why finally—however far in the future—perfection itself should not be attained.

WHAT IS LIFE

If MAN, the whole man, only originates in nature, how is it that he has needs which nature cannot satisfy? If he is born of nature, how can it be that he is in such revolt against nature? And born in uncertainty, how has he ever come to imagine the absolute?

Man is a conscious being: if he is born of nature, and only of nature, it must follow that consciousness exists in nature. Nature, therefore, even in its lowest stages of evolution, must possess, no matter how feebly, some awareness of itself. If man is a creature apart, living by God's will, his consciousness comes to him from God and all is simple. But if man is no more than the end product of a material evolution within a closed cycle, when and how did consciousness manage to enter his being? Either there is no consciousness anywhere except in man—in which case man's origin is not the same as that of matter—or else there is consciousness everywhere.

Consciousness is a fact as a tree is a fact. We are so constituted that we cannot conceive of ourselves except as conscious beings. When we speak of man's immortality, we mean the immortality of his consciousness; when we speak of man's resurrection, we mean the resurrection of his consciousness. But where does consciousness reside, where does it come from, what is it? Does it exist in man alone, is it man's exclusive possession? For, once again, it is self-evident that if consciousness is not exclusively a human characteristic, it must exist everywhere: in animals, in plants; even lodged somewhere deep in the molecules of stone and, still deeper, in the constituent parts of the atom. For if one follows the theory of contemporary physics, the constituent parts of the atom are imponderable; they are not matter, yet they become matter. The atom is spirit, yet acquires weight; it is invisible, yet can be calculated; it may only have a mathematical existence, yet man photographs it. We are in the presence of a point at once so minute and so far beyond human measurements that its apparent contradictions and discrepancies can almost be said to have been reconciled.

It seems obvious that the materialistic viewpoint, by claiming that man is wholly matter and at the same time that there is no consciousness in matter, becomes involved in a basic contradiction. This classic materialism believes, or used to believe, that matter was inert and could only be moved by outside forces, that matter had weight which you must lift and set in motion, that matter did not lift itself nor set itself in motion. But today a revised materialism reaches entirely different conclusions. The forces which yesterday surrounded the atom are today inside the atom. Today it is no longer a question of the river sweeping along the grain of sand, for now the river's motion is merely a mild offshoot of the prodigious, but captive motion contained within the grain of sand itself. The truly great forces are now found to be internal and motionless, or seemingly motionless, because they are imprisoned in themselves, condemned to move in a closed circuit, and when man desires to use them, he needs only to disrupt this immobility, to put an end to this inner balance, to interrupt the ordered rotation—like putting a stick in the spokes of a wheel.

It is in the atom itself, or in its component parts, that the great forces of nature dwell. The immobility of the atom is made up of extreme

motion; the greater the immobility, the more perfect the stability, the more rapid the motion. The
atom only acquires weight because it revolves
upon itself; the more elements it contains, that
is, the faster it whirls, the more it weighs. Then
why, in the last analysis, should not this motion
be conscious of itself? For here is the real problem. And, furthermore, if there is consciousness
everywhere in nature (and it is impossible not to
concede this, once you accept the evolutionary
hypothesis which excludes an act of God), would
it not be perfectly logical to endow consciousness
with the same attribute of immortality which scientists grant to matter? Would it not be even
more logical to grant this same immortality to
consciousness in the loftiest manifestations of
matter among which, however imperfect he may
be, man is surely the most lofty?

The conscious human being is nature's masterpiece. How could nature, which refuses to sacrifice its basic elements—the atoms themselves
which we cannot imagine disappearing—be willing to sacrifice the masterwork, the human being,
the conscious human being? Is this not what
Goethe was saying, a little obscurely no doubt, in
a conversation recalled by Eckermann: "Never,
under any circumstances, could nature allow

such a vital force (he is speaking here of man) to disappear. Nature does not spend its capital with so prodigal a hand."

The classic school of materialism said: "Nothing lasts," and of course man felt the emptiness first in his heart, but his reason also remained unsatisfied. Let us suppose for the sake of argument that matter is merely the product of chance. How can human reason accept this fact? For human reason exists, and is only conscious of existing because it establishes an order of its own, an order completely opposed to the anarchy of chance. Reason sees that matter, evolving slowly and laboriously, reaches its apex, its crowning achievement, in the human being—and then it sees that the human being is the first of these achievements to be cast back into nothingness. There again human reason is at a loss to understand. Reason, contemplating the universe, sees itself dedicated to the one task of trying to create some sort of meaning within a meaningless universe. But reason then realizes that the validity of any meaning it can establish is only momentary in the long night of a meaningless eternity. So human reason asks itself: "How can it be, in the midst of meaningless matter, that man himself is capable of seeing a meaning?" Matter has no goal, though all goals are possible to it; but man has a goal. How does it happen that, in the universal anarchy of chance from which man springs, he should have a sense of logic; that, in the universal disorder, he should be enamored of order? And then man asks: "How can I have been given the ability to reason by nature, which lacks all reason? What is the connection between chance and order, both of which exist, yet are diametrically opposed? How can I love anything beyond what exists; how can I desire anything beyond what happens; how can I, who am foredoomed, aspire to survive forever; and destined to suffer, how can I hope to cease suffering?"

If the universe, the whole universe as we know it, originated in a primitive nebula once immobile and then set in motion, it is not impossible to conceive of a time when that motion will cease, since motion that once began must also have an end. (But what first set the nebula in motion?) And indeed it is the usual materialist viewpoint that motion sustains irreversible and continual losses and must therefore come one day to a stop. Hence the inevitable conclusion is universal death, the nullification of all motion through the complete stabilizing of the constituent parts of matter. It so happens, however, that if immobility is accepted as a terminal point, it must also be accepted as a starting point. No materialistic theory can alter the fact that if motion ceases it must once have started, nor the fact that this motion must in some manner be outside the body it moves. It therefore follows that matter either has resources unknown to us and, because of its vastness, finds a way to perpetuate motion beyond reach of all our machines (which are so small a part of matter, though we imagine that they reproduce the forces contained in matter)—or else there is a God, a God outside matter, a transcendent God. If there is a God, then matter must be animated from outside itself; there must be a Creator; there must be a Person, not just an undefined thing. There must be a Person with intent, with will, with a goal.

If God once created this world as it is, could He not create it once again—and as He wanted it to be? In other words, could He not order His creatures to stand before Him (for with this hypothesis, everything becomes possible) and be judged in some great Last Judgment, and then could He not start creating anew, I mean creating another universe—not just this universe, the one we know? And if there were not a transcendent God, there might still be an immanent God, a force in the depths of the universe itself, a force as yet entirely unsuspected which would raise the dead world from its death and, after casting it into nothingness, would create it again out of nothing.

In any case the nihilistic view of the world is not logical. It claims that matter is eternal, but that motion, which animates matter, is not eternal. Theology, on the other hand, claims that there is matter and there is soul, there is matter and there is God. Since it is impossible to say that motion will last forever unless you say that it has always existed, the theologian reasons, logically enough, that motion is eternal because it exists in an eternal God. Whether or not matter has this same eternal life is of slight importance: matter is merely a sheath or covering, a weight, or even a hindrance. Matter is apt to pull us down, and we must keep thrusting it aside if we are to advance. Matter is forced on man's consciousness, at least during his life on this earth, but he might some day conceivably be freed of it without any lessening of his consciousness— since consciousness is everything while matter is nothing. This intellectual position is obviously clear and, once you grant the heart's participation in it, once you accept a pre-existing faith, it is not unreasonable.

The hypothesis of the immanent God, in which matter and motion are both considered eternal, is also logical. All that is needed to establish its truth is scientific proof, which is lacking; but even without scientific proof, man's intelligence can more easily accept this solution than the one which abandons the universe to a hopeless evolution into final nothingness. For our reason accepts without difficulty the idea that matter is after all not inert; it is easy to conceive that motion may be inherent in matter and even that matter is motion itself. We are only prevented from accepting completely the idea of perpetual motion, in other words, the idea of perpetual life, by certain gaps in scientific demonstration: for example, no experiment has ever succeeded in proving that a steam hammer, under certain conditions, could return by itself to the position from which it falls; or that a steam engine could keep its heat just as inevitably as it fails to keep it.

225

Our reason is only faced with contradiction on a strictly experimental plane, a plane limited by our meager resources for conducting experiments, but the real question goes far beyond this limited plane. It is a metaphysical question and it involves the whole universe. Science itself cannot reach a conclusion; moreover true science, it must be admitted, does not attempt to conclude. But science does not satisfy man's needs.

Science does not even satisfy the scientist, I mean the scientist as a human being, as a man, for problems of detail only have a meaning for man when their solution brings him a step closer to the solution of the entire problem of his life. The scientist sees in part; the human being within him demands to see the whole.

That need for the absolute which the scientist, as such, rejects because the longing to know the unknowable seems to him absurd, nevertheless returns so constantly to plague him as a human being that, despite his wish to explain the world in terms of *how,* he is driven to investigate the *why.*

The concept of a total void does not dismay the scientist, for it lies beyond the limits of scientific research; but the idea of nothingness so preoccupies the scientist as a human being that he is continually tempted to deny or proclaim it.

It is ironic to observe that the scientist almost never ends up with a philosophy representing his own conclusions, a more or less legitimate transposition of the results of his discoveries to the metaphysical plane. On the contrary, the scientist most often starts out with his own philosophy. I mean that before the scientist undertakes his research, he is already equipped with a concept of the world, a concept of which he is more often than not quite unaware, since it is merely the expression of his own particular nature, physiology and temperament. He then spends the rest of his life attempting to convince himself that what he originally believed is the objective result of his research.

Thus there is a major quarrel between the mechanistic scientists who deny God and what we might call the vitalist scientists who believe in God. It might not be too difficult to show that they are both primarily defending their own individual bent. For some men are prone to believe in the concepts which abet and fortify their natural emotions (a phrase of Claudel's fits such men: "Where there is the most joy, there is also

227

the most truth") ; but there are other men who put their pride and bitter pleasure in forfeiting, in the name of reason, all that might content the longing heart.

What staggers the imagination is that man should be so constituted that his encounter with the world he lives in, so far at least, has led only to the most hideous confusion.

What staggers the imagination is that the world should be so little comprehensible, and man so ill-equipped to understand it that, so far at least, he has only seen it as a series of flagrant contradictions.

If man is the product of this world, how does it happen that this world is so completely alien to his understanding? If man is not the product of this world, if he comes from beyond it, from somewhere else, how does it happen that he is so completely helpless?

The world, with its sky, light, night, seas, fields and mountains, reveals itself plainly enough, you would think. Yet you have one man for whom the world contains one God, another for whom it is filled with many gods, and still another for whom it holds neither God nor gods:

the same world contains many gods and no gods at all.

The world is darkly mysterious to man and man is darkly mysterious to himself. Man does not understand himself; as for the world, it is not even conscious of itself, or at least we have no way of knowing whether it is or not. For the world is silent, while man speaks; but the silence of the world cloaks no more mysteries than man's speech, for man, who aspires to knowledge and claims to know, has only an inconsistent smattering of knowledge.

Is man still too young? Is he merely a helpless child? Indeed, it looks as though the whole progress of his mind has served only to multiply the questions which he cannot answer.

What staggers the imagination most is that man can never stop contradicting himself and contradicting his neighbor, that he is not only profoundly split within himself but also split from his neighbor, and therefore continually driven to warfare, even to actual battle—and all his wars are fundamentally wars of belief.

If man were truly the product of this world, he would not question it. He would simply live. The bird simply lives; so, too, the squirrel, the hare and the whale. Why must man seek an explanation of the world and, if he must, why then does he show himself so unequal to the task?

So many religions, so many philosophies, so many scientific theories, and despite them all, man sees that he knows nothing.

He may perceive ever more clearly the *how* of things, but this does not really interest him, and he gains in perception of the *how* at the cost of perceiving ever less clearly the *why* of things, which is his passionate concern.

And what has ordained it so? Is it a force, or a Person? Is it chance, or is it God, the "hidden God" of the Scriptures?

But even to this question no living man can give an answer unless he has a faith, for he can know only by first believing; in other words, he does not know, but he believes.

Ah, if it were the heart alone that mattered, if we could only be sure that Claudel was right when he said: "Where there is the most joy, there is the most truth!" The heart is quick to identify with truth whatever pleases it, and with reality whatever is ennobling. The heart thirsts for the absolute and it is only one step further to conclude that the absolute exists.

But in this debate, alas, what authority can the heart produce, what credentials can it offer? The heart is only a wretched muscle in our bodies; it can only feel, it can only desire to know; but it knows nothing. Doubtless the heart is a part of nature, but reason, too, is a part of nature; and who is to decide between heart and reason? Some men put their faith in reason, others in the heart: who is the final arbiter?

The men of the Right ask themselves whether feeling itself has not its own prerogatives. If the heart is a part of nature, then its longing for an absolute, its longing for survival, for eternity, for immortality, its longing for another plane on which those very contradictions facing us here and now shall at last be reconciled, is natural too. But the men of the Left say that such longings do not exist in nature, or that if they were once natural to man, they are so no longer.

The men of the Left trust in science; therefore they trust in time. For it is by stealing nature's secrets one after another that science will finally succeed in mastering nature. It is through the gradual discovery of nature's creative processes that science in turn will become creative, and use for its own purposes, in its own way, the forces which it has succeeded in capturing and diverting from their natural flow. First, science penetrates, then it exploits. Science justifies itself by its results: the more fruitful the exploitation, the closer it must be to the truth. The fashion among some men (men of the Right) is to disparage applied science, but would it not be more reasonable to admit that these despised practical applications of science are the very proof that science is on the right path? In other words, the more useful science becomes, the closer it is to truth, and the proof that science is in harmony with truth lies precisely in its ability to make man's life easier.

"Stop looking for a God Who does not exist," say the men of the Left, "look how we are driving Him each day a little further out of the universe. The same heart that drew you to God through fear of the material world will draw you back into this world when fear is banished. Look at the people whom we call men of conscience: they live apart; they are solitaries, contemplatives, idlers; in other words, they are useless; or, to put it another way, they are sports of nature, lost to all that is wholesome, and therefore doomed to neurosis, to all the countless forms of hysteria which are, after all, only a deflection into unreality of forces which have found no outlet in reality.

"The real, the true, is relative and we are willing to accept the fact that it is only relative. But in the very heart of the relative we shall create a new absolute. For even the absolute is really only a matter of balance. It is the balance between certain needs and the complete satisfaction of these needs, and we maintain that this world will suffice to establish the balance though it is not everlasting. There is no other world, and just because there is no other world, our main task is to remould the one we have.

"Metaphysical needs are fictitious for the very reason that they aspire to something non-existent and presuppose a dissatisfaction with the world as it is. We must wipe out the contradiction between man's feeling and his reason, for it is this contradiction, allowed to exist by other social systems, which stands as a symbol of their failure. We claim that the day will come when the heart no longer craves something beyond what reason can reveal. We shall have to reeducate mankind; we shall have so to arrange the conditions in which man lives that he will be continually compelled to cooperate with our aims. From his earliest childhood we shall establish his place in collective humanity, for that is where he belongs. Assuming equal rights to all men from the very day of their birth, we shall find a way to arrange human society so equitably that every man will have full scope to work."

The animals are unencumbered by any metaphysics. Are we to be told that the animal has no fear of death? When an animal suffers, it too, like a person, seems to be downcast.

The dread of death may not belong exclusively to man. It is true of course that a busy, healthy man is not constantly preoccupied with the fact that the day will come when he must die, but will it ever be possible to keep men so continuously busy, so completely channelized in their work, so entirely oblivious of themselves, that they never give a thought to death? Will it even be possible ever to preserve men from all illness, to keep them from growing old? Actually, euthanasia is the kind of death which the Left envisages for man, since the Left, not always quite free of pedantry, rather fancies terms that sound scientific. Man must be made ready to die willingly, almost gladly—because of his physiological state. Death has always been so painful because it usually comes while some organs are still intact and others are stricken, and the balance between them is thus disrupted. But will there not be such progress in medicine that man can eventually live on and on until his body is literally worn out(assuming that science finds no remedy for exhaustion)? Will it not eventually be possible, with a simultaneous process of exhaustion throughout man's organism, for him to yield himself wholly, all his body consenting, to a final sleep? In the society of the future and in the millenium it is to entail, we shall see the aged, heavy with years and toil, die in serenity—just as, after a long day's excursion, children fall asleep as soon as they are put to bed.

Meanwhile, however, we must face the fact that old people are unhappy. I assume, of course, that they all have money enough, that they are all loved and respected by their children and grandchildren, and even, if you like, that they are all replete with honors; still, they are unhappy—simply because they are old.

Their misfortune is not due to special circumstance nor is it accidental; it is the direct result of their condition. The aged are discouraged. Look about you, I entreat, look at them carefully, and have compassion on their misery. For they are not merely unhappy, they are miserable, and misery is a step beyond unhappiness. They have no hope. They cannot avoid acknowledging that theirs is a state which can only change for the worse, since they are going down and, no matter what they try to do about it, they can only move downward. They know what awaits them at the bottom and they have no desire for it.

We are all moving toward the same catastrophe as the aged, but they are closer to it. Think of the many '*De Senectutes*' handed down to us by antiquity and of the "Arts of Growing Old" abounding in the literature of ancient and modern times, of all the anxiety they presuppose, the remedies they offer, the consolations of which they are so prodigal—remedies that have never succeeded, consolations that do not console. The old man who is a Stoic, the old man who is an Epicurean, the ascetic, the voluptuary, the old man who still wants to live, the old man who resigns himself to dying: whether they admit it or not, they are all unhappy, they are all profoundly discouraged.

For so many of the aged the painful efforts of a lifetime were devoted to setting aside enough money for a little time of rest upon this earth before being buried beneath it. At last the time has come for them to rest and, too late, they discover that what they have always considered an evil is a good; they always considered their labor a burden, and hoped to be rid of it—but that was before they were free. Now that at last they can rest, they are lost. Here they are, suddenly bared to the wind, with nothing to prop them, nothing left to live for; now they are completely exposed to reality; they are the prisoners of a naked reality which they have never seen before.

It all takes place so swiftly: they had built themselves a little house, they scarcely have time to see the walls dry out and then they die.

They had just finished planting the rose bushes and were already imagining themselves free to putter about with a pipe and pruning scissors, with nothing to do but enjoy themselves as proprietors of a house and a garden. But what are these sharp pains in the side, these sudden twinges beneath the arm?

Ah, now they know, at long last they know what it means to be at rest: that the small difficulties so easily overcome no longer shield them as before from the chief difficulty—to stay alive; because they themselves were small, their little difficulties had hidden the greatest one of all. Now, suddenly, they face the true danger (an unaccustomed danger, since, all their lives, they were preoccupied with the economic dangers which now no longer threaten them); this true danger is death, and they cannot understand why they must die, since they no longer know why they live.

So they wither and change. Everything seems to reject them, for even inanimate objects can give them no pleasure when they themselves have nothing left to give. Even inanimate objects do not speak to the heart, if the heart has nothing to say. The old people asked for little enough: to be outdoors in the sunlight, to read the papers, to smoke a pipe, to listen to the radio, to do some gardening—but even these modest wishes prove too ambitious. Poor creatures, the truth is that they no longer have an appetite for life. Theirs was a false hunger which suddenly failed them, as all false hungers do, and left them gaping in bewilderment at the short time they know is left. By their anxiety about it, they make it shorter still, for in their sudden fright they cry: "It is the liver!" or they cry: "It is the heart!"

Ask the medical men if our illness does not start in the spirit and then creep into the body; or if it does not originate in the higher regions of matter and then spread downward. It is the disease you fear that strikes you: for every idea tends to materialize. Thus the aged who fear death come to die. Their occupations in earlier life, however mechanical, kept them from thinking about themselves; now they no longer have these occupations and they think unendingly about themselves. They see that they are nothing. They see their own nothingness ahead of them and hasten toward it. The fear of dying drives them into death.

Is it not because life as we know it cannot possibly suffice unless we give it a larger meaning, unless we embellish it, even with conscious artifice, but to the best of our ability? We cannot live fully, we cannot be content, until we have bellied out the sails of life with all our illusions, our dreams and our hopes.

*

As I write these lines, Easter is coming and all about me the world of organic matter is coming to life again. At an uneven pace, with sudden growth and pause and growth again, nature is emerging from the state of quiescence in which it was to a new state of flowering which it has not yet fully entered; it is rising from death into life. In the light of the morning all things are hastening eagerly toward life, urged on by the magnetic rays which draw them. Everywhere is song where song had ceased; and in the garden, thrusting themselves between two clods of earth, rose-colored, fragile and vigorous, mysterious new shoots appear. More tenuous and fragile than a thread, each shoot is less yielding than a bar of iron; you need scarcely touch one to see it break off between your fingers, yet if you lay the heaviest stone upon it, it will either lift or cleave the stone, for nothing can resist its strength.

Certain words should not be spoken, for fear of "using them in vain." One should never speak of God, even when one believes in God; one should never speak of the soul, even when one believes in the soul.

Nor should one ever speak of poetry, even when one believes in poetry. It is out of this same reticence that the peasants do not use the word "love"; they say "friendship," which is a lesser word; they use a smaller word in order to leave more room for the thing itself, being shy but in awe of it.

They dare not use the word "love" and it might be better to emulate them; but how can one quell the word, when love abounds everywhere, when everything is bursting into bloom to proclaim it, when everywhere love is manifest? How can one banish it from a discourse which treats precisely of the things that radiate from the heart of love? It is too fine, too large a word; we have a way of standing off from it, or gazing up at it, as though it were beyond our grasp. It must first be reinstated in all its humility, for in this way its real grandeur will be reinstated too. We have given the word a Sunday-like significance: we must make it a weekday word again, for it is an everyday word, a word to be used at all times. We have made love into a kind of symbol, whereas it exists as a fact; we have set it up as a goal, whereas it is the starting point. We have established love in one particular place; but love cannot be thus confined, for it is everywhere. It is not a thing apart from the world, nor somewhat above it; it is here within the world, within the ordinary, everyday world. There is love in everything: in matter, in the heart, in the soul. Not only man is affected by it, but also the animal; not only animals and men, but also plants; not only plants, but also minerals; and not only organic life, but also inorganic life; for all three kingdoms are affected by love. There is no way of avoiding the word, since the thing it stands for is disseminated from top to bottom, from bottom to top. It is in the star, in the pebble, in the flower, in the eye of a cat, and on the mouth of a woman—for its nature is to attract and then to fuse. It is the one-and-one that makes two and the two, which despair at first at their separateness, but are then, however briefly, drawn to each other and by the mutual gift of themselves make one. For, as Saint Bernard has said: "Amor magis est ubi amat quam ubi animat." Then, because each is transmuted into the other, together they become something new.

If the world is nothing but energy, and therefore spirit, as we are told; if energy creates mass, and therefore matter—then the world is nothing but motion. But love has a special part in this motion. It is the quality of the motion. It is its creative quality.

Observe how the scientist who turns his gaze from the star to the atom finds the star again in the atom. Astounded by what he sees, he is forced to recognize the fact that two things so diametrically opposed in size are yet profoundly alike in essence.

The scientist discovers that something infinitesimal can be essentially akin to something vast. He turns his mind from the firmament to the innermost secrets of matter, piercing the ether by which matter is encompassed, for matter must be encompassed by something since there cannot be nothing; and guiding his mind through the maze of the known and the unknown, he comes back to this earth of ours, a little round earth, so insignificant in comparison with the spaces where his mind has traveled, yet so gigantic in comparison with such of its inhabitants as the mosquito, the flea, the microbe. But the scientist does not stop here. He sends his mind spiraling downward through this world of dimensions still further, for while he can see the mosquito or the mite with his naked eye, he cannot see the microbe. He has succeeded in gradually enlarging the power and range of his vision only by a series of inventions, by devising the magnifying glass to divide and then subdivide, to make from the original particle of dust an infinity of such particles, and from each of these still another infinity. But there is a limit beyond which the eye, even with artificial aid, cannot see; yet if the eye despairs of seeing further, the mind, man's mind, can out-distance it, for while the eye has been extending its line of vision, the mind, too, has developed. At each increase of vision, the mind has taken possession of the eye's new powers and adapted them to its own uses, so that when the eye is no longer of any avail, the mind can take over. The mind advances where the eye can no longer follow. The eye was still able to perceive the cell and beyond the cell, the molecule; but it is the mind that has discovered the atom and, penetrating to the heart of the atom, has discovered the miracle itself, for though at first the atom was thought to be indivisible we now know that it can be split. The atom itself becomes a universe, and the fragments of the atom have as much room to move within it as the planets within their system. The atom is quick, it is complex, it lives; even the atom is inhabited by love.

Love, if it exists at all, is everywhere. It is in matter, in the heart, in the soul. Matter itself is procreative. It is a gathering together of particles, themselves composed of smaller particles, which whirl round and round a common center. As they revolve, they make a wall for the atom—in other words, for the family of particles—a wall so thick as to seem impenetrable from either side. Yet for all that, one of the children—one particle of the atom, one member of the family— suddenly manages to escape. Some other love has spoken, some love outside the circle. Suddenly one of the particles of electricity breaches the wall, compelled by another love (as it happens in human families) ; it escapes from the circle (does this not conform exactly to what we call the "family circle"?) and, yielding to an overwhelming force, escapes from its family, only to create another. This is of course an offense, but a flaming offense, since it serves to illuminate the world.

There are conflicting loves, various centers of attraction competing with each other; there are continual eruptions and it is these eruptions which illuminate the world. For there is a world in balance which is dark, and there is a world out of balance which is alight. The world is both dimension and passion. The balanced world is measured in dimensions, while the unbalanced world is measured in passions. Is not attraction, as the word is used in physics, a kind of passion? That love "which sets the moon and stars in motion" also controls the atom and the motion of its planets, for planets have their own procreative impulse and so has the atom, at least at its heart. There is nothing more truly animal, more truly human, than those "opposites," as the scientist calls them, the positive and the negative impulses attributed to the particles within the atomic system, if, as we believe, these opposites are drawn to each other, complement each other, and come together in an embrace, the male with the female, from which something new is born. The procreative impulse is at the beginning of everything and at the end of everything, and so love, too, may be said to be beginning and end. Therefore there is no beginning nor any end because, when all is ended, there is still love, the eternal rebirth.